SELF-IMITATION IN THE
EIGHTEENTH-CENTURY NOVEL

Self-Imitation
in the
Eighteenth-Century
Novel

MARIE-PAULE LADEN

PRINCETON UNIVERSITY PRESS

PRINCETON, NEW JERSEY

Copyright © 1987 by Princeton University Press
Published by Princeton University Press, 41 William Street,
Princeton, New Jersey 08540
In the United Kingdom: Princeton University Press,
Guildford, Surrey

Library of Congress Cataloging in Publication Data will be
found on the last printed page of this book

ISBN 0-691-06705-8

Publication of this book has been aided by a grant from
the Whitney Darrow Fund of Princeton University Press

This book has been composed in Linotron Granjon

Clothbound editions of Princeton University Press books
are printed on acid-free paper, and binding materials are
chosen for strength and durability. Paperbacks, although
satisfactory for personal collections,
are not usually suitable for library rebinding

Printed in the United States of America by
Princeton University Press,
Princeton, New Jersey

To my mother

CONTENTS

ACKNOWLEDGMENTS   ix

NOTE ON TRANSLATIONS   xi

INTRODUCTION   3

CHAPTER ONE
Gil Blas and *Moll Flanders*: Imitation, Disguise, and
Mask   23

CHAPTER TWO
Pamela, La Vie de Marianne, and *Le Paysan parvenu*:
Self-Imitation—The Appearance of Reality   69

CHAPTER THREE
Tristram Shandy: Imitation as Paradox and Joke   128

CONCLUSION   156

APPENDIX   163

BIBLIOGRAPHY   175

INDEX   189

ACKNOWLEDGMENTS

My interest in the French and British Enlightenment was awakened by a seminar on eighteenth-century fiction taught by Robert Scholes and Arnold Weinstein at Brown University. I should like to thank them for letting me participate in stimulating discussions when I was not yet regularly enrolled as a student at Brown.

This study originally took shape under the direction of Arnold Weinstein, whose own work and generous comments on mine were always an inspiration to me. I should also like to express my gratitude to the late Reinhard Kuhn, and to Suzanne Nash and Alban Forcione, whose encouragement and exhortations finally convinced me that my study was worthy of publication.

Above all I wish to acknowledge my debt to Jack Undank, who read two versions of this manuscript with a scrupulousness and sympathy that far exceeded duty, and with a keenness of perception that has helped shape my own aspirations as a scholar. His criticism proved as intriguing and constructive as his other suggestions.

Other debts are to Faith Beasley, who typed an early version of this study; to Olivia Farrar Wellman, who spent many hours incorporating revisions into the original manuscript, improving the quality of the English, checking the quotations, helping with the translations, and typing the final copy; to Darla Rudy, who was of great help in incorporating the final revisions and compiling the index; to Marilyn Campbell, of Princeton University Press, for editing the manuscript so meticulously; to my colleagues who have taken an interest in my work; to Princeton University, which furthered my research by providing travel grants for study in France, and which granted me a leave of absence in the spring of 1982.

ACKNOWLEDGMENTS

Last but not least, I thank my husband, Richard Laden, who, although allergic to Marivaux's style, assisted me in translating the quotations and read the various versions of this study, even when doing so imperiled domestic peace.

Princeton, New Jersey
May 1986

NOTE ON TRANSLATIONS

Translations of passages marked with lettered notes appear in the Appendix. Translations from *Gil Blas* are adapted from *The History of Gil Blas of Santillana*, translated by Henri Van Lann, revised and completed by Henri Roberts (Philadelphia: The Bibliophilist's Library, 1898). All other translations are my own.

SELF-IMITATION IN THE
EIGHTEENTH-CENTURY NOVEL

INTRODUCTION

> I will answer for it the book shall make its
> way in the world, much better than its mas-
> ter has done before it—oh *Tristram! Tris-
> tram!* can this but be once brought about—
> the credit which will attend thee as an au-
> thor, shall counterbalance the many evils
> which have befallen thee as a man.
>
> Lawrence Sterne, *Tristram Shandy*

WHETHER ONE traces the origins of the novel back to
antiquity, or places its genesis as recently as in the
eighteenth century, the history of the novel begins with first-
person narratives. In books 9 to 12 of the *Odyssey* Ulysses tells
his own story to the Phaeacians. Slightly closer to our time, Petronius's *Satyricon* and Apuleius's *Metamorphoses* (*The Golden
Ass*) are also told in the first person. Although the Middle Ages
witnessed the apotheosis of the epic in which the privileged
pronoun is the third person, Boccaccio and Chaucer, among
others, often use the first person in their tales. But the prosperity of the first-person novel dates back to the seventeenth
century in Spain, with the birth of the picaresque novel.

Early writers of novels relied on the first person since they
sought to imitate preexisting genres such as letters, confessions, memoirs, or journals. (*Lazarillo de Tormes*, for instance,
is a letter Lazarillo addresses to his protector.) In eighteenth-
century France and England the novel, as opposed to the more
"authentic" forms of nonfiction had a bad reputation.[1] Hence
the obligatory preface or editor's note that accompanies each

---

[1] See Georges May's *Le Dilemme du roman au XVIIIème siècle* (New Haven: Yale University Press, 1963).

eighteenth-century novel, assuring the reader that what follows is not fiction, but a "true" story.[2]

But the authors' desire to set the seal of authenticity upon their works is not the sole explanation for the popularity of the first-person narrative form. One need not have read Alain Robbe-Grillet's or Michel Butor's novels to realize that the use of the first person in a novel is the result of a conscious aesthetic choice, that a story is not the same told in the first person as in the third. We might also explain the popularity of first-person narrative in the eighteenth century by a property specific to the form: namely, the double character of a narration in the first person, the variety of possible modes of interaction between the "I" acting within the story and the speaking or writing "I." As Emile Benveniste describes the two levels of first- or second-person discourse (which he distinguishes from the "nonperson" or third-person form),

> 'je' désigne celui qui parle et implique en même temps un énoncé sur le compte de 'je': disant 'je,' je ne puis ne pas parler de moi. A la deuxième personne, 'tu' est nécessairement désigné par 'je' et ne peut être pensé hors d'une situation posée à partir de 'je'; et en même temps, 'je' énonce quelque chose comme prédicat de 'tu.'[3]

The significance of Benveniste's comments lies not in the mere duality of enunciation and utterance itself. Even a narration in the third person is both content and discourse, and although the speaker or writer may never be directly impli-

---

[2] See Philip Stewart's *Imitation and Illusion in the French Memoir Novel, 1700-1750* (New Haven: Yale University Press, 1969).

[3] " 'I' refers to the person speaking and implies at the same time an utterance about 'I': in saying 'I,' I am unable not to speak about myself. In the second person, 'you' is necessarily referred to by 'I' and cannot be conceived of outside a situation based on 'I'; yet at the same time, 'I' 's utterance is based on 'you.' " Emile Benveniste, *Problèmes de linguistique générale*, vol. 1 (Paris: Gallimard, 1966), p. 228.

cated by the pronoun "I," any number of other signs of the act of speaking or writing can creep into a supposedly anonymous account. Lacking these, the reader may still be able to draw conclusions about the narrator or the narrator's presumed reader from the point of view, internal consistency, or cultural background of the narration. In other words, even a third-person narrative is not reducible to its referential content; it is also the instrument of a social act, in which someone speaking or writing within a given situation of enunciation is linked (communicates, in a broad sense) with an implied addressee in a particular situation of reception.[4] While all narrative is both enunciation and utterance, the fact that the "I" of first-person narrative must serve as the subject of both makes possible certain effects alien to third-person narrative.

These two subjects are logically entwined, with the speaking or writing "I" a product of the experience it relates, and the situation of enunciation an outgrowth, culmination, or plausible extension of the life the "I" recounts. (Theoretically, of course, there is no reason why the logical filiation could not move in the reverse direction, with the "I" speaking in the future tense and anticipating events that lie ahead.) It is not necessary for the "I" as depicted in the story to be completely identical with the writing or speaking "I," or for its adventures to lead inexorably to the circumstances of the enunciation. Perfect identity is in fact impossible, and in the instant that the word "I" is uttered, its content is as severed from its origin and abandoned by the speaker as a bottled message cast into the ocean. Barthes was one of the first to dramatize the fate of the first-person narrator: "When a narrator (of a written text) recounts what has happened to him, the 'I' who recounts is no

---

[4] For a useful study of the ideological implications of the use of first-person and third-person narration, see Susan Lanser's *The Narrative Act: Point of View in Prose Fiction* (Princeton: Princeton University Press, 1981).

longer the one that is recounted."[5] Apart from this fundamental non-identity, we expect differences between the "I" of the past and the "I" of the present, attributable to maturation and experience. There must be enough similarity, however, for the reader to accept the "I" as referring to the same individual at different points in time.

Anything that vitiates this kernel of identity leads to paradox, of a sort that cannot be rationalized without some metalinguistic intervention or interpretation. "He fell ill and died" is an unexceptional detail in a narration, whereas "I fell ill and died" signals that the narration is a joke, or that the usual rules of plausibility derived from real life must be temporarily relaxed. Such a narrative element violates a condition of possibility in the link between enunciation and utterance. The paradigm of impossible assertions of this type (which includes Epimenides' paradox of the Cretan declaring, "All Cretans are liars") is the sentence, "This statement is false." It demonstrates that a conflict between a reference to the enunciation and the content of the utterance can arise even without use of the first person. Given the double-valued "I," however, self-contradiction can easily come about, and entire narrations can be suspended on paradox. One example is the science-fiction story about a time-traveler who, journeying into the past, kills an ancestor or alters the past in some other manner to make impossible the future world he left. A supposedly more serious example is Mallarmé's "Mimique," as analyzed by Derrida in "La double séance."[6]

Such specimens are not just amusements for logicians or rare narrative teratologies. They represent one extreme of the

[5] Roland Barthes, "To Write: An Intransitive Verb?" in *The Structuralists: From Marx to Lévi-Strauss*, ed. Richard De George and Fernande De George (New York: Doubleday/Anchor Books, 1972), p. 169.

[6] See "La double séance" in Jacques Derrida, *La Dissémination* (Paris: Seuil, 1972), pp. 199-257.

semantic axis "same" versus "other," as applied to the enunciation and utterance. That is, enunciation and utterance always stand in some relation to one another, and this relation may range from total conformity and confirmation (a perfect harmony and transparency of signs, of the sort envisioned in medieval theology) to total antagonism. Because of this scale of possibilities first-person narration offers unparalleled richness: we have to ascertain what lies behind the "I" of the enunciation, and whether there is any unity with the subject of the enunciation; we have to determine whether there is any consistent identity associated with the "I" that designates the protagonist of the story; we have to see to what extent the "I" of the enunciation is compatible with the "I" of the story; and lastly, we must come to understand what role this corroboration or contradiction plays in relation to the general thematics of the story. In some texts total conformity might be a fundamental semiotic principle, echoing the clarity of a divine Logos; in others, cacophony might reign, accompanied by playful polysemy or tragedies of thwarted communication.

In addition to explaining the popularity of first-person narrative in the eighteenth century by a need to shore up the credibility or acceptability of a disreputable genre, we might therefore suspect that eighteenth-century writers and their public were drawn to the variety of possibilities inherent in the use of the first person, and particularly to their flirtation with paradox. The central thesis of this study is, in fact, that first-person narratives in eighteenth-century literature represent collectively a systematic exploration of what is often called the philosophical "problem of the subject" in its relationship to signification, and that these narratives are literary expressions of what we recognize elsewhere as the rococo style of the period. Roger Laufer, in particular, has pointed out how the rococo style in art has its literary equivalent: "le trait général de ce style est de réunir avec élégance, par la simple force de leur contraste, des éléments opposés."[7] Paradox is the aim of the rococo; Laufer speaks of "la mise en question, caractéristique du rococo, par l'étonnement, le recul, le doute puis le sourire"; "le sujet réel et énigmatique n'est pleinement suffisant que s'il se borne à une mise en question."[8] The apparent subject can even dissolve into an implicit but mystifying "centre de projection non figuré," like the subject of the enunciation. We do not have to find a framework of paradox in a work to discern the rococo influence. Even in texts that seem to take redundancy and literalness—that is, compatibility—as their governing principle, consistency can be forced or parodic rather than spontaneous. It may display a self-consciousness, or at least a consciousness of combinative possibilities, a disingenuousness, typical of rococo style.

This "mise en question" of the subject that we find in both rococo art and literature is articulated in eighteenth-century philosophy. Eighteenth-century thought attempts to mediate between definitions of the self as Cartesian consciousness or as the empiricist flow of sensations. What often results is the "centre de projection non figuré" Laufer finds in rococo art and literature: a virtual subject, or locus-subject, surprising in its modernity. (Certain ideas of Condillac strikingly prefigure Benveniste's, as we shall see shortly, and certain motifs of the period resemble key images of Freud's in *The Interpretation of Dreams*.) Developing an internal or formal motivation for the prevalence of first-person narratives in the eighteenth century need not require ignoring literary or social history. The formal argument, with its literary, aesthetic, and philosophical con-

---

[7] "The general character of this style is to combine opposing elements with elegance, through the simple force of their contrast." Roger Laufer, *Style Rococo, style des "Lumières"* (Paris: José Corti, 1963), p. 48.

[8] "Rococo's characteristic questioning, through the use of surprise, distancing, and doubt followed by a smile"; "The real and enigmatic subject is sufficient unto itself only if it restricts itself to a questioning." Ibid., pp. 30, 26.

8

text, leads us to ask what social forces are responsible for these intellectual preoccupations: why the problematics of the subject, as we see in philosophy, or the taste for paradox in rococo art and literature. Although we can at most simply acknowledge this question here, it is perhaps relevant that what discussions of social forces in this period primarily center on, the emergence of a bourgeois elite, is itself a kind of paradox.

On the whole, however, questions of social and intellectual history lie outside the scope of this study. In the novels we shall examine our focus will be on the content of the "I"; not just on the division between the writing "I" and the "I" that designates the protagonist, but also on those divisions within the self that seem to herald the "je est un autre" of Rimbaud's "Lettre du voyant" or Valéry's "L'individu est un dialogue."[9] I have chosen to call a first-person novel one in which the agent of the narration is within the narration itself (for example, *Moll Flanders*, as opposed to, say, *Tom Jones*, in which the narrator does not belong to the world of the text). This definition corresponds to what Genette calls a "récit homodiégétique."[10] But since it would also include a novel like Dostoyevsky's *The Devils*, in which the narrator functions as a character in the novel but is not its hero, I have adopted an additional criterion. In all the novels to be considered, the subject of the enunciation, as semiotics would phrase it, is identical with the principal subject-actant of the enunciated; in other words, the narrating "I" and the "hero" of the text are the same person. In Genette's terminology these novels are "récits autodiégétiques."

Most novels written in the first half of the eighteenth century in France and England were fictive autobiographies. Especially notable are Lesage's *Gil Blas*, Marivaux's *Le Paysan parvenu* and *La Vie de Marianne*, Defoe's *Moll Flanders* and

[9] A still earlier exploration of these divisions is the dialogue between Guzmán and Guzmanillo in Alemán's *Guzmán de Alfarache*.

[10] Gérard Genette, *Figures III* (Paris: Seuil, 1972), p. 251.

Roxana, Smollett's *Roderick Random*, and, later in the century, Sterne's *Tristram Shandy*. In the wake of Richardson's *Pamela* (1740) and *Clarissa*, the epistolary novel became extremely popular both in England and in France (not to mention other European countries). Examples include Crébillon's *Lettres de la Marquise* and *Lettres de la Duchesse*, Smollett's *Humphrey Clinker*, Fanny Burney's *Evelina*, Rousseau's *La Nouvelle Héloïse*, and Laclos's *Les Liaisons dangereuses*, as well as most of Restif's novels.

Since my purpose is not to write a history of the first-person novel in the eighteenth century,[11] but rather to analyze the various functions of the first person in narrative and the possibilities it offers, the corpus of this study will be limited to *Moll Flanders, Gil Blas, La Vie de Marianne, Le Paysan parvenu, Pamela*, and *Tristram Shandy*. These few titles illustrate the experimental and as yet unformed state of the novel in the eighteenth century. They represent the vogue of the fictive autobiography, of the travel novel, of the diary, and of the epistolary novel. For reasons that will become obvious, we shall omit the satirical novel.

Except in the diary and the epistolary novel, in which it is usually assumed that the "I" of the protagonist and that of the narrator coincide,[12] the narrator in all these texts is substantially older than the protagonist. This age gap between the narrator and the hero offers several possibilities. There is a difference between the voice of error of the young Moll and the voice of experience of the older woman, a distinction only partially veiled by an apparently single "I." The discourse of the protagonist and that of the narrator can also be juxtaposed or woven together, as in *La Vie de Marianne*, where we witness a

---

[11] It has been done by René Démoris for France, in *Le Roman à la première personne* (Paris: Armand Colin, 1975).

[12] I hope to show in the chapter on *Pamela* (a representative of both forms) that this is not really the case.

10

perpetual shuttling back and forth between the present of the narrator and the past of the protagonist, resulting in the transformation of the past into the present of the writing "I." Although *Tristram Shandy*, in which we witness a writer watching himself write, is the paradigm of self-reflexive writing, similar introspection is also present in the earlier novels. In short, in all these texts the complexity and indirect nature of the first person is usually concealed from both enunciator and listener (or reader) because of its self-referential nature. Ultimately the first person always conceals a hidden third person.

These features of the use of the first person in eighteenth-century fiction will be the principal object of this analysis, but related facets of the works will also be explored: voice and perspective, in particular, but also that which lies outside the self. Most novels of social ascension take the form of fictive autobiography in the eighteenth century. The social themes so often associated with the form require us to explore not only the reflexive aspect of autobiographical writing but also the aspect of the self and the other, the self and society. Primarily, however, we shall be asking to what extent can the self explore itself, not only as the enunciated "I" or protagonist but also as writing "I" or subject of the enunciation? To what extent can the self account for the workings of its memory and for its need to write? How can it do so and portray, through memory and writing, its society, when the impulses of memory and writing themselves arise from a historical or social condition? Given a philosophical coloration, the question becomes how the self comes to consciousness. In regard to the narrators of the works, we might ask more simply what are the individual's motives—conscious or unconscious—for writing his or her autobiography.

It might be objected that this question confuses the narrators, mere literary constructions, with living historical beings. Yet it is easy to exaggerate the difference between "real" and "fictional" autobiographies. It is often assumed that the main difference lies in the role played by memory in "real" autobiographies, versus imagination in fictional texts. It seems to me, however, that the mixture of truth and fiction is next to impossible to determine in either case. The experience of reading Rousseau on Jean-Jacques greatly resembles, from a literary point of view, that of reading Sterne on Tristram. Because of social as well as literary considerations, reading Fanny Burney's journal differs little from reading Fanny Burney's *Evelina*. As Northrop Frye explains, both fiction and autobiography involve selecting, ordering, and integrating the writer's lived experiences according to certain imperatives of imaginative discourse.[13] In other words, both forms transform facts into artifacts, and distinguishing between an autobiography, employing fictions intended or unintended, and an autobiographical novel can be very difficult. In any case, if the narrator, even as a purely literary construction, is to have coherence and logic, surely his or her motivation for writing must be a part of that logic. All the characters we shall consider feel obliged to justify themselves: Moll's reasons for writing are moralistic; Marianne and Pamela are seeking recognition; it seems that Tristram will stay alive as long as he writes, and since he is unable to keep pace with time, his writing earns him a kind of immortality. Behind these reasons, however, lie others, often more subtle or surprising. It is interesting to notice that the discrepancy between these characters' alleged reasons for writing and their unconscious motives parallels the schism dividing the subject of the enunciation and that of the statement: a gap that is occulted by the seeming unity of the "I."

I assume that all these characters create themselves through writing. Writing about oneself is always an affirmation of

[13] Northrop Frye, *Anatomy of Criticism* (Princeton: Princeton University Press, 1957), pp. 107-108.

12

power; it reveals a desire to recompose as much as to discover the self. Again drawing the line between fictive and real autobiographies is difficult, if we consider that all the main characters examined in this study express a need to authenticate their lives by setting them down. Yet their search for authenticity does not preclude contradictions that betray frequent distortions. In fact, once written, the story of a life acquires a status that escapes categorization as truth or fiction, just as it escapes its writer. It is as much created fiction as chronicle of fact. All the texts I have chosen to analyze deal, either transparently or indirectly, with writing as an activity.

By the prominence they give writing, the works we shall look at suggest questions that can be articulated within a more analytical framework. Why does a person aspire to the unity of the authorial "I"? What must be affirmed, exposed, captured, or repudiated by writing? What link exists between the desire to write and other forms of struggle for unity or expression in a person's life? What does it mean for the self to explore the self and its relation to others? Ultimately, one must wonder whether in writing the self is revealed or actually manufactured.

This study is therefore a convergence of several lines of thought. One is the linguistic inquiry associated with Benveniste: the attempt to determine a semantic content for the first-person grammatical form, and the distinction between the "I" speaking and the "I" designated in discourse, investigations that inevitably overstep the bounds of linguistics and acquire a philosophical dimension. A second line is more openly philosophical, even metaphysical, in that it represents an investigation of the nature of the self and an examination of being in general. The third line of thinking ponders the nature of writing. Woven together, these threads of analysis form the problem of the relationship of the self to language. At issue is how

13

language serves the existence of the self, and whether its role is one of presentation, representation, or generation.

What the following readings and analysis will make clear, I hope, is that these preoccupations are not extraneous to the eighteenth-century novels under study, grafted anachronistically onto them by the meddlings of a twentieth-century critical obsession; rather, they are central to an understanding of the works, and involve questions raised with various degrees of explicitness by the works themselves. Both the problems and the conceptual tools with which I approach them have roots in eighteenth-century thought.

As hinted at earlier, for instance, Barthes's comment pointing out that the narrating "I" cannot be confused with the "I" who figures in the narration recalls Condillac's definition of the term *moi*: "Ce qu'on entend par ce mot, ne me paraît convenir qu'à un être qui remarque que, dans le moment présent, il n'est plus ce qu'il a été. Tant qu'il ne change point, il existe sans aucun retour sur lui-même qui a été auparavant de telle manière, et il dit *moi*."[14] Condillac's definition of the self is very modern in its establishment of identity as a yoking of difference and repetition; it also illustrates the eighteenth century's preoccupation with the problem of the subject or the "self," a preoccupation not without links to the contemporary flourishing of first-person narratives. As Stephen D. Cox expresses it, "nothing is more common in eighteenth-century literature and philosophy than the search for the 'true self,' a self that is often rather conveniently regarded both as an individual's 'real' identity, and as the principle from which he can de-

---

[14] "What I believe is meant by this word, seems to me to apply only to a being who notes that, in the present instant, he is no longer what he was. So long as he does not change, he exists without any possibility of return to his earlier self which was of another nature, and so he says *I*." Etienne de Condillac, *Oeuvres philosophiques*, ed. Georges Le Roy (Paris: P.U.F., 1947), 1:238. Quoted by Jean A. Perkins in *The Concept of the Self in the French Enlightenment*, (Geneva: Droz, 1969), p. 54.

rive the greatest moral significance. Yet this essential self proves very difficult to discover and express."[15] This notion of an "essential self" derives primarily from Cartesian thought, and beyond from the philosophy of Aristotle. Yet the works examined in this study demonstrate that while Richardson's or Marivaux's characters may occasionally refer to their "true self" or their "moi," their need for social approval is so strong that it problematizes this very belief in a center.

The Cartesian *cogito* did not solve the problem of the subject for most philosophers of the eighteenth century. Descartes's assertions concerning man's innate ideas were called into question even by the end of the seventeenth century, with the publication in 1690 of John Locke's *Essay Concerning Human Understanding*. Locke's empiricism proved as influential as Descartes's philosophy in the eighteenth century's attempts to determine the nature of the self.

The empiricist tendency of the period was notably championed by Hume. His conception of man as "nothing but a bundle or collection of different perceptions which succeed each other with an inconceivable rapidity, and are in perpetual flux or movement,"[16] had a strong impact on French philosophy. Condillac's famous example of the statue capable of sensation in isolation from the structure of the organism as a whole ("son moi n'est que la collection des sensations qu'elle éprouve, et celles que la mémoire lui rappelle"; "its 'I' is but the sum of the sensations it experiences, and those that memory brings back to it") is strongly reminiscent of Hume's definition. Particularly interesting in Condillac's theory is his insistence on the role of memory. For most philosophers of the

[15] Stephen D. Cox, *"The Stranger Within Thee": Concepts of the Self in Late Eighteenth-Century Literature* (Pittsburgh: University of Pittsburgh Press, 1980), p. 7.
[16] Quoted by Cox, ibid., p. 16.

15

period, memory is essential to the knowledge of the self,[17] a view exemplified by Buffon's comment: "Ce sentiment intérieur qui constitue le *moi*, est composé chez nous de la sensation de notre existence actuelle, et du souvenir de notre existence passée."[18] Insistence on memory as the ultimate foundation of the self appears as a common denominator in an otherwise variegated array of philosophical conceptions of the self, ranging from the belief in a stable center, through that of a bundle of perceptions, to that of an amalgam of both. In d'Alembert's terms, "La notion abstraite d'existence se forme d'abord en nous par le sentiment du *moi* qui résulte de nos sensations et de nos pensées."[19] The self arises, as it were, in some undefined zone between center and periphery: it emerges from a fusion of Descartes and Hume or Locke, from "sensations," by a sort of centripetal movement of collection, but also from "our thoughts," by an outward radial movement of propagation or dissemination.

The metaphor of the spider's web that recurs in eighteenth-century writing is emblematic of the period's perplexity in defining the self.[20] According to one's religious or philosophical beliefs, one could emphasize either the role of the center or that of the periphery of the web. As Georges Poulet expresses it, "La toile d'araignée est formée par un réseau périphérique qui capte et s'annexe un certain nombre d'objets. Mais elle est faite aussi d'une centralité animale et intelligente, où ces ob-

[17] Cf. Voltaire's *Traité de métaphysique* and *Questions sur l'Encyclopédie*, Helvetius's *De l'homme*, d'Holbach's *Le Système de la nature*.

[18] "This inner feeling that constitutes the 'I' is compounded of the sensation of our present existence and the memory of our past existence." Georges-Louis Buffon, *Oeuvres philosophiques*, ed. Jean Piveteau (Paris: P.U.F., 1954), p. 332. Quoted by Perkins, *Concept of the Self*, p. 48.

[19] "The abstract notion of existence arises primarily in us from the perception of the self that results from our sensations and thoughts." In *Eclaircissements* (1767). As cited by Perkins, *Concept of the Self*, p. 44.

[20] Cf. Diderot's *Le Rêve de d'Alembert*, or Montesquieu's *Essai sur les causes qui peuvent affecter les esprits et les caractères*.

jects se trouvent métamorphosés en sensations et en idées. L'image saisissante qu'elle offre est celle d'un monde externe périphérique, incessamment ressenti et repensé par une conscience centrale."[21] The image thus can be a vehicle of mediation for expressing that pure empiricism which, developing ideas of Locke, sees the self as an accidental product of the sensory flux, and that current of philosophy which, following Descartes, sees it as a transcendental subject somehow related to a divine Logos.

Both philosophical polarities between which the eighteenth-century understanding of the self hesitates, as it does in this ambiguous image of the web, have their modern counterparts. In my reading of the novels, it is not, I hope, a question of imposing a modern critical framework on eighteenth-century literature. The intent is rather to discern within these works problems that anticipate issues developed in twentieth-century philosophy.

To suggest several such links and situate the critical assumptions underpinning this study, we might say first that the Cartesian influence on the eighteenth century has its most notable modern analogue in phenomenology: the belief in the possibility of an original intuition, a pure consciousness fully transparent to itself, devoid of presuppositions and requiring no other ground of certainty. For Husserl, a method of variation—the eidetic reduction—lets this self know itself and the world, clearing away thickets of facts to pin down general essences; further "phenomenological" reductions lead us back (*reducere*) from the natural world of experience, temporarily

---

[21] "The spider's web is formed of a peripheral network that seizes and appropriates a certain number of objects. But it is also made up of an intelligent animal center in which these objects are transformed into sensations and ideas. The striking image this web offers is that of an external and peripheral world which is incessantly refelt and rethought by a central consciousness." Georges Poulet, *Les Métamorphoses du cercle* (Paris: Plon, 1961), p. 80.

set aside or suspended (the *epoche*), to the world as phenomenon, constituted by the reflecting subject, and from the phenomenal self or "I" to a transcendental subjectivity.[22] The focus upon Being as it manifests itself in phenomena is the further contribution of Heidegger. It is perhaps harder to trace lines of filiation in phenomenological thought than it is to signal points at which Heidegger diverges from Husserl, and more markedly from the Cartesian tradition; nor is the task of establishing and delimiting inspiration or influence easier in the case of later phenomenologists such as Sartre, Merleau-Ponty, or Ricoeur.[23] In general, however, one can say that, for these philosophers, Being does not emerge from language; it is not a creation of the interplay of signs. It may be revealed within language, as Heidegger shows, or essences may be fixed by language, as they are for Merleau-Ponty, but—at least at privileged moments, or given the proper shift of attitude— Being is simply present to the consciousness of a unitary, stable self.[24] The literary criticism based on a system of thought fall-

[22] Cf. Richard Schmitt's "Husserl's Transcendental Phenomenological Reduction," *Philosophy and Phenomenological Research* 20 (1959-60), 238-45.

[23] For an illuminating collection of essays on phenomenology and the phenomenologists, see *Phenomenology, the Philosophy of Edmund Husserl and Its Interpretation*, ed. Joseph J. Kockelmans (New York: Doubleday, 1967).

[24] In the case of certain post-Husserlian phenomenologists, most notably Merleau-Ponty, the self is not stable but mobile, part of a dynamic interaction with its surroundings (cf. Alan Wilde's excellent essay, "Acts of Definition, or Who Is Thomas Berger?" *Arizona Quarterly* 39 [Winter 1983], 312-50). What is new is not the interaction (an idea already developed by Husserl) or even the necessarily limited perspective of the individual consciousness, akin to the constraints bearing on the historicity of *Dasein*. Merleau-Ponty's contribution is the sense of the fragility of that consciousness, beset with ambiguities. Consciousness has to work harder to wrest its certainties from confusion and then guard them. Phenomenological thought is rarely monolithic, and even Merleau-Ponty on occasion defines the real as unity, presence, and plenitude. The centrality and intentionality of consciousness that post-Husserlian phenomenology retains can never really be reconciled with the modern critical notions of a structure without center, and of a textual locus within which inherited structures intersect. Whereas for Merleau-

ing within this tradition can be either a hermeneutics, which aims at elucidating the historical conditions of the particular consciousness and the historical meaning of the phenomena perceived by that consciousness, or else an effort (exemplified in France by Bachelard, Poulet, J.-P. Richard) to collect and generalize images into essence, in a way that conveys the organized sensory universe of a central consciousness.[25]

While such a critical investigation could take the form of a structural semantics, the notion of structure tends to replace the unity of the subject with an uncentered collection of oppositions, inherited from elsewhere.[26] The phenomenologist's view of a stable consciousness and its objects stands in contrast

Ponty perception and experience construct, found, and unify, for the philosophy and criticism discussed below they are merely made possible by and give evidence of preexisting codes, or a provisional and uneasy equilibrium of forces.

[25] There are, of course, other critical approaches inspired by phenomenology, but to the extent that these escape the necessarily quick generalizations offered here, it is principally because their philosophical ground itself represents a departure from the roots and central tendencies of phenomenology. It would take a different study from the present one to inventory the writings directly or peripherally associated with phenomenology and judge in each case their degree of innovation or fidelity to Husserl.

[26] As Derrida has shown for Husserl, the intelligibility of even the most basic phenomenological perceptions rests on a principle of structural opposition and iterability which phenomenology first acknowledges and then covers up. Husserl's method of variation is not really different from Saussure's. Finding affinities and differences by which images can be ordered is done in much the same way by the phenomenological critics as it is by Greimas in studying the universe of Bernanos (cf. *Sémantique structurale* [Paris: Larousse, 1966], pp. 222-56). What irrevocably divides the phenomenologists from the structuralists, as I have indicated above, is the philosophical interpretation of a structure: whether or not it originates in an individual consciousness, or even in the interaction of that consciousness with a fluid world. Sarah Lawall has pointed out this point of connection (and division) between phenomenological and structuralist views in the Introduction of her *Critics of Consciousness* (Cambridge: Harvard University Press, 1968). Lévi-Strauss's concept of *esprit*, which she specifically mentions (p. 15), has occasionally been attacked by structuralist writers as phenomenological consciousness in disguise.

to modern approaches—the most striking example is the philosophy of Derrida—which subvert the notion of a stable self, much as eighteenth-century empiricism once did. Deconstruction, the demonstration of a writer's attempt and failure to achieve a system of thought that is closed and free from self-contradiction, takes what at first appears to be a stable phenomenon and reveals within it the vacillations of a necessary ambiguity; in the process the would-be unitary consciousness is itself sundered, turned back upon itself. In modern criticism the subject's immediate intuition is replaced by a process: a Nietzschean conflict of forces, a Freudian rhetoric of the unconscious, or the transformation and interplay of earlier texts, themselves transforming earlier texts, in a movement that recalls the image of the spider web without the watchful spider in the middle.

Hume seems to anticipate key ideas of Derrida; we can see as an adumbration of *différance* Hume's insistence on our tendency to "disguise, as much as possible, the interruption," to "remove the seeming interruption by feigning a continued being."[27] Hume's vision of consciousness, in fact, seems to prefigure the semiotics of Peirce: it is a theater with "different perceptions or different existences, which . . . mutually produce, destroy, influence and modify each other."[28]

But the opposition between phenomenology and deconstruction sometimes exists within the same work. Even for Husserl, it can be shown—as Derrida has done in *La Voix et le phénomène*, his early analysis of Husserl's *Origin of Geometry*— that the identity of the phenomenon requires the movement of *différance*, which appears in Husserl's discussion as a combination of retention and protention (anticipation). Much of Heidegger's work, too, escapes the charge of "Logocentri-

[27] David Hume, *A Treatise of Human Nature*, vol. 1, ed. T. H. Green and T. H. Grose (London, 1890), pp. 488, 496.
[28] Ibid., pp. 541-42.

cism"—its Logos is the pre-Socratic one, a collection or system of relations. There is an already "Derridean" Heidegger, just as in one reductive view most of Derrida's work is that of a wayward Heideggerian.

Ultimately, however, we cannot avoid an irreconcilable opposition. On the one hand we have the belief in self-evidence, in presence simply revealed to a secure consciousness. On the other hand, we find the idea that there can be no presence, no phenomenon, without iterability; that something is reproducible because it has been defined as such within a code; and that the subject is only a locus or nexus of codes. To the extent that it is necessary to admit an allegiance, the discussions that will follow clearly espouse the second view. Readers conversant with philosophy will perhaps find the framework of analysis used here reminiscent of Heidegger's presentation of how Greeks understood being, appearing, appearance, and becoming.[29] I have deliberately used this Heideggerian scheme, since I feel that it combines, in a form easy to grasp and apply, concepts essential to an understanding of several main features of the novels selected. It is difficult to say anything meaningful about the mask and how it complicates any opposition of truth to falsity without reference to Heideggerian (or, ultimately, Greek) distinctions. These distinctions also offer a model for the relationship of the protagonist to the narrator. In the structural oppositions that underpin my readings (*être/paraître/non-être/non-paraître*) I am, in addition, indebted to Greimas, and the modalization of being which I introduce is perhaps indirectly inspired by his work.

Primarily, however, the works I have chosen seem to me to elude the simplicity of a phenomenological view of the subject. The vital role in them of writing, imitation, or performance introduces a semiotic complexity with which phenomenology

[29] See in particular Heidegger's *Introduction to Metaphysics*, trans. Ralph Manheim (New Haven: Yale University Press, 1958).

21

cannot come to terms. Being, especially the being of the subject, is not simply given; it must be performed, or it is doubled, with one being evacuated to make place for another metalinguistic being, or it may be parasitically undermined, treated as a lure or a joke, or striven for as an ill-defined potential. It is, in general, not one thing revealed, but something not present, or the intersection of many things. The stories of Gil Blas, Moll Flanders, Pamela, Marianne, Jacob, and Tristram are also stories of semiosis, of a mode of signification that comes into being along with the hero's development into a narrator; in them, what comes to inhabit the "I" of the narrator and speak within it is as much an other as a self.

CHAPTER ONE

Gil Blas and Moll Flanders
Imitation, Disguise,
and Mask

> Ce qui est réel au sens du drame, c'est
> l'événement qui se produit maintenant de-
> vant nous. Ce qui est réel au sens de la nar-
> ration, ce n'est absolument pas d'abord
> l'événement raconté, mais bien le fait même
> de raconter.[a]
>
> Käte Friedemann

I N RECENT YEARS autobiographical writing has received considerable critical attention.[1] At issue in much of this discussion is the relationship between "real" and "fictive" autobiography: not the question of a purported author's civil existence, but a matter of taxonomy, of a distinction or kinship supported by formal or esthetic properties. That veracity and imagination can overlap, or appear each in the guise of the other, is clear in such works as Rousseau's *Confessions*, Benjamin Franklin's autobiography, Henry Adams's *The Education of Henry Adams*, or Stendhal's *La Vie de Henri Brulard*, to men-

[1] See in particular a special issue of *MLN* edited by Rodolphe Gasche, "Autobiography and the Problem of the Subject," 93, no. 4 (May 1978); James Olney, ed., *Autobiography: Essays Theoretical and Critical* (Princeton: Princeton University Press, 1980); Paul L. Jay, "Being in the Text: Autobiography and the Problem of the Subject" *MLN* 97, 5 (Dec. 1982), 1045-63; John Eakin, *Fictions in Autobiography: Studies in the Art of Self-Invention* (Princeton: Princeton University Press, 1985), among other important works listed in the bibliography.

23

tion but a few autobiographical works. Even a casual reader of Rousseau's *Confessions* is struck by the literariness and structural harmony of the first book; without systematically questioning the author's honesty, one may wonder where the boundaries lie between art and the recording of a life, the *récit*. To what extent does Rousseau's factual truth depend on art to make its impression, and is it in any sense less true for this dependence? Conversely, many critics assume art imitates life, or is even a kind of translation of life. For instance, they seem unable to refrain from drawing a parallel between the narrator of a novel and the "real" author of the work. For many readers of *Moll Flanders*, Moll's "casuistry" only reflects Defoe's.[2] Roger Laufer's view of *Gil Blas*—as a disguised autobiography of Lesage himself[3]—also illustrates this tendency to treat the narrator of fictive autobiography as the author in costume. As a result, one might be tempted to lump all autodiegetic texts together in the same corpus and to analyze them under such headings as "Autobiography Considered as Fiction," or "Fiction Considered as Autobiography," or "Fiction in the Form of Autobiography," and so on, according to the reader's mood and inclination.

Philippe Lejeune tries to distinguish between "fictive" and "real" autobiography by positing that in any "real" autobiography the "I" of the narrator-protagonist must correspond to the name of the author printed on the title page of the book.[4] Though it carries all the leadenness of a tautology, this idea is

---

[2] See for instance, G. A. Starr's *Defoe and Casuistry* (Princeton: Princeton University Press, 1971).

[3] Roger Laufer, *Lesage ou le métier de romancier* (Paris: Gallimard, 1971), p. 288: "Lesage introduisit l'unité vivante et changeante de sa propre personnalité dans un roman qui devint en partie une autobiographie déguisée."

[4] Philippe Lejeune, *Le Pacte autobiographique* (Paris: Seuil, 1975). "Le pacte autobiographique, c'est l'affirmation dans le texte de cette identité (auteur-narrateur-personnage) renvoyant en dernier ressort au *nom* de l'auteur sur la couverture," p. 26. See also pp. 23-24.

certainly not incontrovertible. Its flaws are both philosophical and procedural. For one thing, its "reality" is limited: the name used as the antecedent of the "I" in the book is the same one used where one customarily finds the author's name. The coincidence promises no greater truth; an autobiographer could very well bestow another name on the protagonist-narrator in the most accurate and straightforward chronicle of events, just as we might encounter the same name in a story that diverges wildly in its factual or emotional content from the author's own life. If the occurrence of the same name marks "real" autobiography, we might well ask from the philosophical standpoint whether a reality limited to this vacuous homonymy is at all meaningful. Furthermore, Lejeune's touchstone has the drawback of imposing a factual rather than esthetic test to determine the genre of a literary work, on an only slightly higher plane as it were, than weighing the book or measuring the type font.

More seriously, it fails to address the real question. Does it really matter whether the "I" of the narrator refers to a flesh-and-blood person or not? Even though the names may be the same, and notwithstanding a writer's declared resolution of making a faithful rendering of life, any translation of physical experience into the condensed medium of written narration alters its character irrevocably. Life exists, with its signs and perceptions; and writing exists, with its signs. Between these two systems of signification or experience, there is at most a relationship of suggestion or signification: not an identity. Nor can an author who professes literal translation avoid having the mode of telling the story shape the perception of the teller. Certainly a vow of transparency is not to be trusted; it normally accompanies the most tendentious and self-serving of narratives. In short, there is no real identity between the "author" of a text and the author as perceived by what one might call his narratee. For this reason it might be more fruitful to address the problem of autobiography from a linguistic perspective, and ask what composes the "I."

Any first-person narrative, including the novel, necessarily represents a constellation of selves. The "I" can never be joined seamlessly to a real author or a set of historical circumstances, and this is so whether the "I" refers to a fictive character or not. Not only is there a gap between thought and language—between the depth of lived experience present to a writer's mind and the experience of signs and writing (perhaps almost as rich or ramified, but with a different sort of profundity) within which the reader constructs an antecedent—but there is also the separation between the memory or experience of the event itself and the event of narration. Like Proust, or Augustine and Montaigne before him, Rousseau was aware of this ambiguity: "En me livrant à la fois au souvenir de l'impression reçue et au sentiment présent je *peindrai doublement* l'état de mon âme, à savoir au moment où l'événement m'est arrivé et au moment où je l'ai décrit" (my emphasis)[5].

Linguistics skirts complexity; from the standpoint of this discipline, what lies behind the "I" is clear-cut, but little enhances our understanding of a literary text. Benveniste's statement that " 'je' est l'individu qui énonce la présente instance de discours contenant le mot 'je' "[6] rightly points out that the pronoun "I" (or "you") refers only to a reality of discourse. The real question, nevertheless, is whether we can ever say anything more than this about the "I," or whether the speaking or writing self is, paradoxically, forever condemned to an-

[5] "In surrendering myself to both the memory of the initial impression and my present feeling, I shall *paint doubly* the state of my soul, namely at the moment events happened to me and at the present moment when I am describing them." Jean-Jacques Rousseau, *Oeuvres autobiographiques* (Paris: Gallimard, 1959), p. 1154.

[6] " 'I' is the individual responsible for the present discourse containing the word 'I.' " Benveniste, *Problèmes*, p. 252.

onymity even as it tries to introduce itself. From the literary standpoint it is discomfiting to see in the "I" a mere role without an identity. It is, rather, natural to dissect the pronoun "I" (or "you") to try to determine—by implication or logical presupposition, drawing upon the form and content of the discourse that is the narrative—who the "individual" is that Benveniste mentions in his definition.

The present chapter will consider Lesage's *Gil Blas* and Defoe's *Moll Flanders* from the perspective of the enunciation. I am therefore concerned with these novels as discourse as well as story. Unlike the many critics who choose to remain at the level of the story (*histoire*) and see in the use of the first person mainly the author's desire to enhance the illusion of reality, we will concentrate on Moll's and Gil Blas's attitudes toward their stories. We should steer clear of two opposing errors: treating the narrator as an extension or mouthpiece for the actual author, so that the story is overshadowed by life itself; or treating the story as one might any narrative in the third person, and ignoring the quality and function of the narrator's discourse. Between these fallacies is another approach, which is to treat the narrator both as the protagonist within the story, and as a speaking or writing "I" that must be studied and, in effect, reconstructed from the circumstantial evidence of the discourse. (The narrating "I" can obviously lie in speaking of itself, but we learn something if we can trap it in contradictions.) We confer a peculiar autonomy upon the narrator, a status that must be regarded as a heuristic device or critical fiction. If we allow for some inevitable blurring of the distinction between the two roles of the narrator—the same name must serve for both the speaker/writer and the main character—this approach recalls Bakhtin's. As early as 1928 Bakhtin founded his analysis of Dostoevsky's novels (which he termed "dialogical") on the independence of the hero vis-à-vis his author: "The hero's consciousness is given as a separate, a foreign consciousness, it is not made the single object of the author's consciousness." . . . "The hero's word is created by the author, but created in such a way that he can freely develop its own inner logic and independence as the word [*slova*] of another person, as the word of the hero himself."[7] Not much time should be spent debating whether Defoe or Moll is responsible for any irony that may exist in the novel. This does not mean that the novel should be attributed to a fictitious character who is part of it, but rather that one should refuse to ascribe to the author what belongs to the character. Or rather, since the realm of autobiography forces us to be more finicky than Bakhtin, we should avoid confusing the author or the protagonist with the "I" responsible for the discourse.

Examining two novels as different as *Gil Blas* and *Moll Flanders* in the same chapter might seem strange at first. They are, of course, linked chronologically (they were both written early in the century, 1715/1735 and 1722) and literary-historically (they are usually considered as influenced by the classical Spanish picaresque). They also have in common their autodiegetic nature. What unites them more profoundly, however, is how the picaresque themes of imitation and disguise create not the usual flat world of the picaresque, but—as we shall see—an inner necessity, a dynamic within both the protagonist's personality and the narrator's discourse. The mask becomes not just the standard instrument of deceit in a round of *tromperie*, but the philosophical mainspring, the condition of being of both hero and narrator. Since it does so somewhat differently in each novel, a comparison of the two works gives a fuller sense of how the mask bonds the story to the discourse.

On the surface, the narrative voices are quite different. Gil Blas and Moll have divergent attitudes toward their earlier selves. In the case of *Moll Flanders*, the gap existing between

[7] Mikhail Bakhtin, *Problems of Dostoevsky's Poetics*, trans. R. W. Rotsel (Ann Arbor, Mich.: Ardis, 1973), pp. 4, 53.

the two voices—the young Moll's voice of innocence and the narrator's voice of experience—is narrower than in *Gil Blas*. As we shall see, the narrator, despite her moral pose, is hardly any more fixed or settled as a character than was her younger picaresque avatar. It is as if the narrator becomes a double of the young Moll, as if the "I" represents not a mature Moll, as one would expect, but a psychological accomplice of her younger self. Yet her similarity is not identity; in fact, it reminds us that she is neither exactly the same as the heroine nor her true successor. The contradiction between complicity and moral posturing that we find in the narrative voice has its correlative in the story. A similar dichotomy is visible in Moll the protagonist. For instance, the scene in which the elder brother seduces Moll features a division between young Moll's sensual nature and her susceptibility to manipulation by abstractions such as money and status. A further difference between the two narrations is that Moll's "I" is more obtrusive than Gil Blas's. It seems at times that Moll has to convince herself as well as the reader of her honesty, whereas Gil Blas makes it clear that his present prosperity is the result of an innate inclination toward virtuous behavior.[8] Consequently, the two narrators' attitudes toward their narratee are fundamentally distinct; Gil Blas's confident affirmation does not seem to need the reader—to implicate the reader in the narration—as much as Moll's uneasy apologia.

The most obvious consequence of the use of the first person in a narrative is the temporal gap existing between the protagonist's voice of error and the narrator's voice of experience. The gulf is seldom as wide as in *Gil Blas*.[9] As opposed to Moll,

---

[8] It is significant how often Gil Blas does the right thing when he is offered the choice, as when he saves Dona Mencia (Book 1), and how he congratulates himself for doing so.

[9] The gap between narrator and protagonist is comparable in Crébillon's *Les Egarements du cœur et de l'esprit* in which Meilcour's wit and irony

Marianne, Jacob, or Tristram, who constantly intermingle their present "I" with that of their younger selves, Gil Blas the narrator keeps his distance from the protagonist he once was. For this reason it is often assumed that Gil Blas is not a real character, that he is merely a device used to string together all the episodes of this *roman à tiroirs*: "Ainsi les événements ne s'enchaînent pas: ils se succèdent. ... Les vies humaines, de même, se rencontrent, s'éloignent, sans se pénétrer, ni réagir l'une sur l'autre."[10b] A short glance at the table of contents reinforces the impression of detachment; although Gil Blas uses the first person to refer to himself in the text, the third person or the hero's name is used in the titles of the various chapters. The striking contrast between Marianne's "je conte mon histoire" and "De la naissance de Gil Blas et de son éducation," illustrates how all elements of reflexivity tend to disappear in Gil Blas's tale.

Many readers conclude that his novel reads like a book written in the third person, especially since Gil Blas is not always the object of his own story—there are hundreds of interpolated stories in the novel, told by other characters and merely reported by the narrator. Marie-Hélène Huet thus writes that "Gil Blas narrateur donne curieusement l'impression d'écrire à la troisième personne."[11] This statement holds true for the last section of the novel—paradoxically, here, where the temporal or psychological distance between the narrator and the hero vanishes the formal distance becomes greatest—but *Gil Blas* as a whole could not have been written in the third person without becoming a totally different book. Let us

spring from his emphasis on the distance between what he was and what he has become.

[10] Lesage, *Histoire de Gil Blas*, ed. Maurice Bardon (Paris: Garnier, 1962), p. vi. All subsequent references will be to this edition.

[11] "Gil Blas as narrator gives the strange impression of writing in the third person." Marie-Hélène Huet, *Le Héros et son double* (Paris: José Corti, 1975), p. 25.

examine an early passage in the book, in which Gil Blas talks not about himself but instead about his uncle and educator Gil Perez:

C'était peut-être (car je n'avance pas cela comme un fait certain) le chanoine du chapitre le plus ignorant: aussi j'ai ouï dire qu'il n'avait pas obtenu son bénéfice par son érudition; il le devait uniquement à la reconnaissance de quelques bonnes religieuses dont il avait été le discret commissionnaire, et qui avaient eu le crédit de lui faire donner l'ordre de prêtrise sans examen. (Book I, p. 4)*

Though such a passage written entirely in the third person might still keep its irony, it would lose all its humor. The narrator's fake uncertainty ("c'était peut-être") only emphasizes his detachment and self-assurance; it is very different from Moll's uncertainties. And the narrator's irony is often directed against himself, that is, against his self of many years ago. In the following passage Gil Blas recounts one of his adventures on the road; the innocent Gil Blas easily falls prey to the fraud who is buying his donkey:

Alors, faisant l'homme d'honneur, il me répondit qu'en intéressant sa conscience je le prenais par son faible. Ce n'était pas effectivement par son fort; car, au lieu de faire monter l'estimation à dix ou douze pistoles, comme mon oncle, il n'eut pas honte de la fixer à trois ducats, que je reçus avec autant de joie que si j'eusse gagné à ce marché-là. (Book I, p. 7)*

Here the narrator's irony is of course directed against the dealer, but more importantly, emphasizing the naive protagonist's joy at the moment when he is being bamboozled enables him to display his talents as a writer—as in the antithesis *faible/fort*—at the protagonist's expense. In similar instances throughout the first ten books of the novel, the narrator implicitly passes judgment on the world, while his self-mockery lets him distance himself from the protagonist. But the attitude of the narrator toward Gil Blas the character is not always so oblique. He often frankly condemns his past attitude: "Que j'étais fat, quand j'y pense de raisonner de la sorte" (Book 4, p. 250).[e] No extradiegetic narrator could make such remarks about characters without overinterfering in the story; the deictic "quand j'y pense" would have to be omitted, resulting in: "Qu'il était fat de raisonner de la sorte."

The literariness of Gil Blas as a narrator is striking. His delight in puns, his mastery of dramatic irony, as illustrated in the above quotes, allow him to flaunt his superiority over the protagonist. In the picaresque world of appearances and conventions, factual truth is never an adequate response in a social situation, and in his encounters with others, young Gil Blas always meets trouble when he innocently attempts to tell the naked truth. This predicament is illustrated in his various dealings with innkeepers: "Je demandai une chambre, et pour prévenir la mauvaise opinion que ma souquenille pouvait encore donner de moi, je dis à l'hôte que, tel qu'il me voyait, j'étais en état de bien payer mon gîte" (Book 1, p. 53).[f] To corroborate his words Gil Blas shows his thousand ducats to the innkeeper, who soon finds a way to transfer them from Gil Blas's pocket to his own. The narrator gleefully exposes the simplicity of Gil Blas's language and actions. Naively impulsive, they function entirely at the literal level, taking the world at face value.

A favorite target for the narrator's irony is Gil Blas's ill-digested reading. As opposed to most picaresque heroes, Gil Blas is learned, and his literacy will prove to be one of the mainsprings of his social success. So imbued is he with literary grandeur that when misfortune strikes, Blas tends to burst into mock-heroic, high-flown speeches which the narrator delights in contrasting with the sordidness of his situation. Upon becoming a prisoner of Rolando and his gang Gil exclaims: "Oh ciel! dis-je, est-il une destinée aussi affreuse que la mienne?" (Book 1, p. 24);[g] and later, " 'O vie humaine!' m'écriai-je quand je me vis seul et dans cet état, 'que tu es remplie d'aventures bizarres et de contretemps!' " (Book 1, p. 45),[h] upon finding himself in prison after telling the truth. The narrator pokes fun at the verbosity of these "réflexions futiles" and obliquely opposes them to his own wit and linguistic efficiency. Such contrastive comments have generally been overlooked by critics; Stuart Miller, for instance, alleges that "just as the character of Gil Blas is submerged in his novel, so is the narrator."[12] It is true that in *Gil Blas* the relationship between the narrator and the protagonist is, on the surface, less ambiguous than in *Guzmán de Alfarache* or *Moll Flanders*, since it is often difficult to distinguish between the various voices in the latter two books; yet Gil Blas is not more "submerged" in his story than other narrators, precisely because of the ironic distance maintained between the narrated event and the speech event through most of the book. The narrator hardly seems submerged in the following instances: "Au lieu de n'imputer qu'à moi ce triste incident, et de songer qu'il ne me serait point arrivé si je n'eusse pas eu l'indiscrétion de m'ouvrir à Majuelo sans nécessité, je m'en pris à la fortune innocente, et maudis cent fois mon étoile" (Book 1, p. 62).[i] "Mais j'étais trop vif pour souffrir des injures dont un homme sensé n'aurait fait que rire à ma place, et la patience m'échappa" (Book 7, p. 6).[j] This "submerged" narrator spells out in detail what course of conduct he would have followed had he been wiser. Elsewhere he casts doubt on the purity of the protagonist's motives: "D'ailleurs, Eufrasie ne m'avait rien promis de positif, et cela peut-être était cause qu'elle n'avait pas corrompu ma fidélité" (Book 4, p. 249).[k]

[12] Stuart Miller, *The Picaresque Novel* (Cleveland: Case-Western Reserve University Press, 1967), p. 117.

Not only is the narrator irreconcilably estranged from his former self, but there is a radical split between Gil Blas as he sees himself—or rather, as he wants the reader to see him—and as he finally emerges in his memoirs. The nature of this split is apparent on closer examination of young Gil Blas's career. If writing is by definition an important activity for the narrator, it is no less so for the protagonist: it becomes the instrument of his success, and through it he climbs the social ladder. After keeping the books for Doctor Sangrado Gil Blas becomes a copyist for the Archbishop of Granada, who praises his handwriting as well as his knowledge (Book 7, pp. 11-14). After this modest beginning he becomes the Duc de Lerme's private secretary, entrusted with texts to edit. Later Gil Blas works for the Comte d'Olivares, the next prime minister, who asks him to write a report presenting the minister as the savior of the nation: "Santillane, me dit-il, je ne t'aurais pas cru capable de composer un pareil mémoire. Sais-tu bien que tu viens de faire un morceau digne d'un secrétaire d'Etat?" (Book 11, p. 283).[1] In this brief summary of Gil Blas's "literary" career the emphasis is on praise of his style and literary capacity. In the light of the speech event (*discours*) rather than the narrated event (*histoire*), it appears that the enunciator or narrator is reenacting his past successes as he writes. There is no irony here; on the contrary, the narrator is retrospectively savoring his various masters' compliments along with the protagonist. But what is interesting here is the discrepancy between what the narrator wants to convey—what a success he was—and the ultimate effect of such passages. The reader realizes that success comes about not by any true achievement on Gil Blas's part—he is, after all, not an original writer—but arises from the impact elegant imitation produces on those around him. What precedes the above quote is illuminating in this respect: "J'entrai si bien dans les vues du nouveau ministre qu'il fut tout surpris de mon ouvrage lorsqu'il l'eut lu tout entier" (Book 11, p. 283).[m] In spite of the narrator's efforts to glorify the protagonist's accomplishments, it appears that his success is primarily due to his skill at guessing what is expected from him.

This adaptability of the hero is in fact the driving force of the story: Gil Blas's ascension can be attributed entirely to his talents as mimic. Lacking a clearly defined identity of his own, in order to survive he must become someone else's reflection, and it is for this reason that Gil Blas is so often looked upon as a passive hero. (According to René Démoris, "Gil Blas manque singulièrement d'invention."[13] Maurice Bardon, who mainly admires the mastery of Lesage's "tableaux de moeurs," is even more severe in his judgment of the protagonist: "Le malheur de Gil Blas, c'est qu'il faille le définir surtout négativement: il est le héros de l'insuffisance."[14]) To be sure, Gil Blas does not show much initiative in the novel, and when he does, he is bound to run into trouble. For instance, when the Archbishop of Granada asks him what he thinks of his latest sermons, Gil Blas trusts his own judgment and candidly answers: "votre dernier discours ne me paraît pas tout à fait de la force des précédents." As might be expected, the archbishop promptly dismisses him from his lucrative job: "J'ai été furieusement la dupe de votre intelligence bornée. ... Adieu, monsieur Gil Blas; je vous souhaite toutes sortes de prospérités, avec un peu plus de goût" (Book 7, pp. 19-20).[n]

Moll Flanders declares her *non serviam* early in the novel and adheres to it; Gil Blas, on the other hand, climbs the social ladder by serving. In spite of his youthful ambition to use his education when he leaves his native town of Oviedo, his friend Fabrice has no difficulty convincing him that the only road to

[13] "Gil Blas shows a striking lack of inventiveness." René Démoris, *Le Roman*, p. 351.
[14] "The problem with Gil Blas is that he can be defined only negatively: he is the hero of inadequacy." Lesage, *Histoire de Gil Blas*, ed. Bardon, p. xv.

prosperity in their world is domestic service. It is he who offers Gil Blas the key to success;[15] significantly, Gil Blas cannot make this discovery on his own, but again must pattern his actions after another's vision.

> Le métier de laquais est pénible, je l'avoue, pour un imbécile; mais il n'a que des charmes pour un garçon d'esprit. Un génie supérieur qui se met en condition ne fait pas son service matériellement comme un nigaud. Il entre dans une maison pour commander plutôt que pour servir. Il *commence par étudier son maître*: il se prête à ses défauts, gagne sa confiance, et *le mène ensuite par le nez*. C'est ainsi que je me suis conduit chez mon administrateur. Je connus d'abord le pèlerin: je m'aperçus qu'il voulait passer pour un saint personnage; je feignis d'en être la dupe, cela ne coûte rien. *Je fis plus, je le copiai; et, jouant devant lui le même rôle* qu'il fait devant les autres, je trompai le trompeur, et je suis devenu peu à peu son *factotum*. (Book 1, pp. 66; my emphasis)[p]

The whole passage deserves to be quoted and analyzed, since the application of Fabrice's precepts will have far-reaching consequences in Gil Blas's career. Fabrice's words also throw some light on our hero's misfortunes in the first book of the novel. When Fabrice claims that the intelligent servant "commence par étudier son maître," he illuminates what has been lacking in his pupil's behavior so far. Things and people are what they appear to be for Gil Blas, owing to his education and his parents' precepts. ("Loin de m'exhorter à ne tromper personne, ils devaient me recommander de ne pas me laisser duper" [Book 1, pp. 10-11], remarks the narrator bitterly.)[p] In a

[15] Fabrice can be seen as a picaresque version of Crébillon's Versac in *Les Egarements*. For a related analysis of the function of imitation in *Gil Blas*, see Marie-Hélène Huet, *Le Héros et son double* (Paris: José Corti, 1975), pp. 14-24.

world of signs, the relationships between the signifier and the signified are fixed and immutable, unequivocal, characterized by the *adequatio* of truth: Gil Blas behaves with others as if they were duplicates of himself, and is predictably and constantly flimflammed by Raphael, Camille, and various innkeepers.

In Bakhtin's terminology, Gil Blas can be classified as a "monological," single-voiced character (that is, not affected by another's word). By substituting a discourse based on the knowledge of the other for a discourse based on the knowledge of the self, Fabrice finds the means to impose his will on the other instead of being imposed upon ("et le mène par le nez"). Having assimilated the rules of the game, he has learned to control by indirectness situations that he could never have manipulated directly: "Je fis plus, je le copiai . . . *factotum.*" Finally, Fabrice emphasizes the importance of role-playing. Instead of reducing others to himself, as Gil Blas does, he deliberately becomes their reflection.

Gil Blas, who is so attached to exterior appearances, is easily convinced: "Je me résolus à prendre un habit de cavalier, persuadé que *sous cette forme* je ne pouvais manquer de parvenir à quelque poste honnête et lucratif" (Book 1, p. 54; my emphasis).[q] As in Marivaux's *Le Paysan parvenu*, dress and discourse are endowed with an independent truth; if he wears the *habit de cavalier*, Gil Blas becomes a *cavalier*, in his eyes as well as in those of others. What distinguishes Lesage's work from Marivaux's is the distance established between the narrator and the protagonist. "Quel plaisir j'avais de me voir ainsi équipé! Mes yeux ne pouvaient, pour ainsi dire, se rassasier de mon ajustement. Jamais paon n'a regardé son image avec plus de complaisance" (Book 1, p. 55).[r] This could very well be Jacob talking, except that in the last sentence the narrator's irony carefully separates what is expressed from the act of utterance.

When Gil Blas takes Fabrice's advice and becomes a ser-

37

vant, his life imitates this copy of a copy. Fabrice is not his only model; Gil Blas first observes his fellow servants, then replicates their attitude toward the master: "Je remarquai avec étonnement que ces trois domestiques copiaient leurs maîtres, et se donnaient les mêmes airs. . . . Ils ne se contentaient pas de prendre les manières de leurs maîtres; il en affectaient même le langage; et ces maurauds les rendaient si bien, qu'à un air de qualité près, c'était la même chose" (Book 3, pp. 150-51).⁵ Here again the discourse of the narrator is quite distinguishable from that of the protagonist. The epithet *marauds* belongs to the utterance act and stands in sharp contrast to the protagonist's admiration for his colleagues' virtuosity. But the narrator's attitude toward the protagonist becomes more ambiguous as the temporal gap between the narrating "I" and the experiencing "I" diminishes.

These object lessons are not lost on the protagonist; he pushes the imitation so far that he even borrows his master's clothes and identity, thus becoming the latter's alter ego: "Il fallait voir comme nous nous portions des santés à tous moments, en nous donnant les uns aux autres les surnoms de nos maîtres ... ils me nommaient de même Silva; et nous nous enivrions peu à peu, sous ces noms empruntés, tout aussi bien que les seigneurs qui les portaient véritablement" (Book 3, p. 152).⁵ The giddiness of the servants is no doubt due as much to the name under which the toasts are drunk as to the liquor itself. If we believe Gil Blas and his colleagues, assuming one's master's identity not only enhances the taste of the wine one drinks, it also raises one's consciousness: "Vois ce que c'est que de servir des personnes de qualité! cela élève l'esprit: les conditions bourgeoises ne font pas cet effet" (Book 3, p. 153).⁶ As a consequence, Gil Blas insists on only serving and imitating noblemen, and does not conceal his contempt for the bourgeoisie, whom he blames for doing exactly what he does himself: "Il affectait en vain de prendre l'allure des petits-maîtres;

c'était une très mauvaise copie de ces excellents originaux, ou, pour mieux dire, un imbécile qui voulait se donner un air délibéré" (Book 3, p. 154)."

Gil Blas's world becomes a hall of mirrors, a succession of images and reflections in which one loses track of the original. When Gil Blas, wearing his master's costume, courts a "lady of quality," he discovers that she herself is wearing her mistress's dress. Fabrice seeks to be a poet, but he only encounters success when he imitates Góngora. Appearance and imitation prevail over essence at all levels of the book. Money, clothes, good food, and vintage wines are not relished as such, but as the signs and manifestations of a particular social status: "et l'on me servit avec des marques de considération qui me faisaient encore plus de plaisir que la bonne chère" (Book 8, p. 90)." Gil Blas's concern with praise and the good impression he makes on others displaces any real zest for life. Indeed, we might question whether Gil Blas lives at all, since he seems to exist only by proxy in his various guises. He is in this respect quite different from the other picaros and frauds he meets in his peregrinations.

What distinguishes a Rolando, a don Raphael, or a Laure from our hero is not so much their lack of moral principles (as the narrator would have us believe), but their willingness to give up respectability and security in order to satisfy their desires. Disguised as a hermit or monk, don Raphael still retains his personality, whereas Gil Blas tends to dissolve under his many masks. Rolando and don Raphael risk the galleys everyday, whereas the presence of Gil Blas's master deflects any sense of responsibility from the protagonist. When he dispatches his patients to their graves it is as Doctor Sangrado's assistant. Whatever the consequences of his acts, Gil Blas is only obeying orders. In this regard the many interpolated stories studding the novel are not superfluous; from a structural point of view they serve as a standard against which the protagonist's progress can be measured. The narrator implicitly blames Rolando's or don Raphael's lack of scruples and morality. By inserting the accounts of their violent deeds in his tale Gil Blas can set off his own innocence all the more strikingly. But the effect of these stories does not conform to his intention: what emerges most vividly for the reader is that don Raphael and others like him act in accordance with the rules of a certain code (even if it is that of brigandry), whereas Gil Blas's acts and discourse have no referent.

The pattern of mimicry established by Gil Blas as a servant is repeated not only in the interpolated stories but also in the general structure of the novel. When we notice that the three parts of the book, published respectively in 1715 (Books 1-6), 1724 (Books 7-9), and 1735 (Books 10-12), all reproduce each other, we realize that opening this novel is like entering an endless hall of mirrors. Moreover, what we read initially copies the story of copying copies, in an unstoppable regression that precludes an origin. Thematically, Gil Blas's experience with the Duc de Lerme is exactly paralleled by his stay with the Comte-Duc d'Olivares. Both men give him various memos to write; Gil Blas then becomes their confidant, and both entrust him with the task of finding a mistress for the crown prince who has become king in the last part. Critics sometimes look upon such recurrences as evidence that Lesage's imagination is drying up, that he is forced to exploit a vein already mined with great success in the first two parts. But when one perceives that this imitative pattern of the novel is paralleled by the imitative function of the protagonist, and picked up once more by the narrator who is reproducing his life through his discourse, it appears as one of the most interesting characteristics of this famous but virtually unread novel.

Lesage is a master of the *mise en abyme*. Within this reflexive framework, in which each event or character refers back to another ad infinitum, Gil Blas is as much a mirror for his masters as they are for him. When the Comte-Duc d'Olivares remarks that Gil Blas seems less corrupt under his ministry than he was under that of his predecessor de Lerme, Gil Blas observes: "le mauvais exemple corrompit mes moeurs: comme tout se vendait alors, je me conformai à l'usage; et, comme aujourd'hui tout se donne, j'ai repris mon intégrité" (Book 11, p. 310).[x] Gil Blas's self-portrait is merely a succession of such metamorphoses. His "identity," therefore, is merely their locus, and the implication of this last quotation is that the picture we get as a result always refers to another. Gil Blas illustrates on the level of the story Benveniste's statement that the first person is a role, that it is in fact (given the temporal dimension of the enunciation) a series or succession of roles brought together under the illusory unity of the "I." *Gil Blas* thus prefigures the conception of the text advocated by French semiotics in the seventies. To the enunciation corresponds the "deep structure" of the text, a process rather than a product; here, we might say it is the imitative principle itself, at work in various places and on various levels of the story. The chain of *énoncés* corresponds to the surface structure, in which meanings are effects (*effets de sens*) produced by the shaping rhetoric or generative principle. In the case of Gil Blas, the guises and disguises of the self are, like such meanings, copies or signs of something else, purely formal effects of a process anterior to meaning.

Such multiplicity, duplicity, and reflexivity of the first person is nowhere so well illustrated as when Gil Blas, still a servant, hires a servant for himself: "Celui-ci paraissait fort éveillé, plus hardi qu'un page de cour, et avec cela un peu fripon. Il me plut. Je lui fis des questions: il y répondit avec esprit; il me parut même né pour l'intrigue" (Book 8, p. 104).[y] From this portrait it appears that the candidate who most appeals to Gil Blas is a reincarnation of himself. He is characterizing himself and his attitude toward his own masters when he describes Scipio. "Scipion, qui me copiait si bien qu'on pouvait dire que la copie approchait fort de l'original. . . . Je ne pouvais voir en lui qu'un autre moi-même" (Book 8, p. 133; Book 9, p. 169).[z]

By the time Gil Blas acquires a servant the book is like a serpent biting its tail. First Gil Blas imitates his masters, so successfully that he identifies with them both physically (borrowing their clothes and names) and morally. Then he too becomes a master, while significantly still remaining a servant. He sees himself in his servant, who in turn imitates him. The major circle is closed, but subsidiary spirals still await development. Consider, for instance, that even Gil Blas's most prestigious masters are themselves servants of the king, whom they have to imitate and to please. They themselves have other servants who also act as mirrors for Gil Blas, such as Calderone, the Duc de Lerme's other secretary. Being as corrupt as Calderone, Gil Blas is unable to judge him, he only sees the image Calderone projects to others:

> "D'un autre côté, j'apercevais des cavaliers qui, choqués du peu d'attention qu'il [Calderone] avait pour eux, maudissaient dans leur âme la nécessité qui les obligeait de ramper devant ce visage. J'en voyais d'autres, au contraire, qui riaient en eux-mêmes de son air fat et suffisant. J'avais beau faire ces observations, je n'étais pas capable d'en profiter. J'en usais chez moi comme lui, et je ne me souciais guère qu'on approuvât ou qu'on blamât mes manières orgueilleuses, pourvu qu'elles fussent respectées. (Book 9, p. 141).[aa]

Although Calderone is a mirror for Gil Blas, the protagonist can only perceive Calderone refracted through others.

It comes as no surprise that the theater and actors should be of paramount importance in this book. The theater reflects the world as much as the world reflects the theater:

Si le marquis, pendant les trois quarts du jour, est, par son rang, au dessus du comédien, le comédien pendant l'autre quart, s'élève encore d'avantage au dessus du marquis, par un rôle d'empereur ou de roi qu'il représente. Cela fait, ce me semble une compensation de noblesse ou de grandeur qui nous égale aux personnes de la cour." (Book 3, p. 179).[bb]

Sentences like, "Vous jouez, à ce que je vois, un assez beau rôle sur le théâtre du monde" (Book 12, p. 319), are merely clichés in most eighteenth-century texts. In Lesage's work they are woven into a web of theatrical metaphors, for example, "Comme un héros de théâtre qui se met à genoux devant sa princesse" (Book 3), or Raphael's answer to his mother who complains about his being a renegade: "Au lieu de vous révolter devant mon turban, regardez-moi plutôt comme un acteur qui représente sur la scène un rôle de turc" (Book 5, p. 306).[cc] The hundreds of figures who appear in the novel, however fleetingly, consciously play some kind of role or strive to project a chosen image. Gil Blas serves an actress for a while before becoming himself an actor; although he is soon dissatisfied with this world of illusion, he only leaves it to play the part of a comedy servant in a gentleman's house: "Songeons au rôle que je dois jouer. . . . Je me rappelais même dans ma mémoire tous les endroits de nos pièces de théâtre dont je pouvais me servir dans notre tête-à-tête, et me faire honneur" (Book 4, pp. 195-96).[dd] And Gil Blas goes on, using quotes from *Le Misanthrope*: "Ah! madame, l'ai-je bien entendu! est-ce à moi que ce discours s'adresse?" (Book 4, p. 197). Though for the reader it is evident that actors function as mirrors, Gil Blas curiously does not recognize himself in them, despite the fact that his world and values are no less illusory than theirs.

All these theatrical references clearly link *Gil Blas* to baroque literature. What Jean Rousset says about literature written a century earlier could serve as an apt description of Lesage's novel: "Tout se meut ou s'envole, rien n'est stable, rien n'est plus ce qu'il prétend être, les frontières entre la réalité et le théâtre s'effacent dans un perpétuel échange d'illusions, et la seule réalité qui demeure est le flot des apparences cédant à d'autres apparences."[16] This lack of a clear-cut line, this constant flow between reality and appearance distinguishes Lesage's use of theatrical metaphors from Crébillon's or, later in the century, from Laclos's. In Crébillon's and Laclos's works, the mask and disguise are deliberately put on in order to conquer; an aggressive self hides behind the mask (see Merteuil's famous autobiographical letter 81 in *Les Liaisons dangereuses*, or Versac's precepts to Meilcour in *Les Egarements*.) Characteristically, in these works theatrical metaphors are subservient to martial images; the successful wearer of masks does not fall victim to his/her role. In *Gil Blas*, on the contrary, as in classical literature, everyone wears a mask in a dizzying play of false appearances. What distinguishes *Gil Blas*, from the baroque literature studied by Rousset is that in Lesage's novel the *trompe l'oeil* never leads to any realization that the self might be in jeopardy.

Mimicry is also the rule among the numerous writers represented in the novel. They ape the nobility in not believing in the value of their art, looking upon their work rather as marketable goods. Fabrice, their mouthpiece in the novel, does not imitate Góngora from sheer admiration for the master: "J'ai si bien pris son esprit, que je compose déjà des morceaux abstraits qu'il avouerait. Je vais, à son exemple, *débiter ma marchandise* dans les grandes maisons où l'on me reçoit à mer-

---

[16] "Everything changes form or disappears, nothing remains what it seems to be, the boundaries between reality and theater dissolve in a continual flux of illusions, and the only reality remaining is a stream of appearances giving way to others." Jean Rousset, *La Littérature de l'âge baroque en France: Circé et le paon* (Paris: José Corti, 1953), p. 30. See also pp. 28, 29, 54.

veille, et où j'ai affaire à des gens qui ne sont pas fort difficiles" (Book 7, p. 61; my emphasis).*ee* One becomes a writer as easily as one becomes a servant: "Je suis devenu auteur, je me suis jeté dans le bel esprit; j'écris en vers et en prose; je suis au poil et à la plume" (Book 7, p. 59).*ff* The world of writers, as represented by Fabrice and his fellows, is another microcosm of the whole novel; thematically and structurally, it is another compartment of this Chinese box. Fabrice and his like also function as mirrors for their masters:

> Par cette complaisance, qui ne me coûte guère, possédant, comme je fais, l'art de m'accommoder au caractère des personnes qui me sont utiles, j'ai gagné l'estime et l'amitié de mon patron. Il m'a engagé à composer une tragédie, dont il m'a donné l'idée. Je l'ai faite sous ses yeux; et, si elle réussit, je devrai à ses bons avis une partie de ma gloire. (Book 11, p. 297) *gg*

There is no need for Fabrice to add that if the tragedy fails it will be his patron's fault. Here again, as in the world of servants, all responsibility is deflected. Characteristically, Gil Blas is blind to the affinity between his vacuous self, a locus of images registered and reproduced, and the writers' world of signs. He mildly despises Fabrice for his activities: "Quels charmes as-tu donc pu trouver dans la condition des poètes? Il me semble que ces gens-là sont méprisés dans la vie civile, et qu'ils n'ont pas un ordinaire réglé" (Book 7, pp. 59-60).*hh*

In the above examples, it is rather difficult to distinguish between the utterance and the utterance act; the discourse of the narrator and that of the protagonist tend to mingle. The irony is directed against Fabrice, the various actors and writers, and it only obliquely reflects on the protagonist. Although the reader may perceive that Gil Blas is only an image of an image's image, just as is Fabrice, there is no indication in the text that the narrator shares this view. As the story progresses, as the temporal gap between the protagonist and the narrator diminishes, the narrator lets the protagonist speak and refrains from criticizing him.

The passage in which Gil Blas has received his *lettres de noblesse* from the king demonstrates a total equality between protagonist and narrator: "Mais lisons-les, continuai-je en les tirant de ma poche; voyons un peu de quelle façon on y décrasse le vilain. Je lus donc mes patentes, qui portaient en substance que le roi, pour reconnaître le zèle que j'avais fait paraître en plus d'une occasion pour son service et pour le bien de l'Etat, avait jugé à propos de me gratifier de lettres de noblesse" (Book 12, p. 333).[ii] Even the irony of the pert remark "de quelle façon on y décrasse le vilain" belongs to the protagonist as well as to the narrator. This is the tone of the last book of the novel, which could be translated into the third person without any modification of its form and content. Although thematically the last part is a perfect replica of the preceding one, the narrator tends to erase himself from his discourse.

Such discretion replaces the narrator's irony toward the protagonist of the first books of the work (for example, "Jamais paon n'a regardé son image avec plus de complaisance"), an irony that itself becomes a systematic requital against his former self in the central part of the novel: "Je *changeai* tout à coup avec la fortune, n'écoutai plus que mon ambition et ma vanité. . . . *Avant que je fusse à la cour*, j'étais compatissant et charitable de mon naturel; mais on n'a plus là de faiblesse humaine, et j'y devins plus dur qu'un caillou" (Book 8, pp. 119-20; my emphasis).[ii] In this middle section of the story, the narrator is the most severe toward his former self, and he manipulates language in such a way as to convey a sense of Gil Blas's native goodness at the same time as he stresses his corruption ("Je changeai," "avant que je fusse à la cour"). The indirect message to the addressee is that the models are more corrupt than the hero, and hence that he is susceptible to cure. In other

words, Gil Blas the writer is paving the way for the protagonist's recovery in Book 9 to become more praiseworthy. For
what characterizes the hero and the narrator most is their
thirst for praise: the former is always fishing for compliments
from his masters, and the latter twists his tale so that the reader
will praise him, too.

This is not the case in the last part of the novel; here narrator and protagonist are equal morally as well socially. The
narrator seems to efface himself in order to respect the objective facts and to let the event speak for itself. His tone is absolutely neutral in the following examples: "Je m'attendais donc
à passer le pas; néanmoins mon attente fût trompée. Mes doc-
teurs m'ayant abandonné, et laissé le champ libre à la nature,
me sauvèrent par ce moyen" (Book 9, p. 172).*ᵏᵏ Even the pique
against doctors—who have been the butt of the narrator's bitter attacks throughout the book—is very subdued. "Scipion
partit donc encore pour Madrid; et moi, en attendant son retour, je m'attachai à la lecture. ... J'aimais surtout les bons
ouvrages de morale, parce que j'y trouvais à tout moment des
passages qui *flattaient* mon aversion pour la cour et mon goût
pour la solitude" (Book 9, pp. 172-73).*ˡˡ One would look in
vain for any trace of irony in Gil Blas's discourse here. The text
is one-dimensional, transparent, and consequently far less interesting than when the hero's actions were commented upon
by the narrator. Note also that there is no attempt on the narrator-protagonist's part to penetrate the meaning of the works
he reads, even in the case of philosophical works. Characteristically, he merely finds in them a reflection of his present
state of mind.

Does this limpidity of the last section of Gil Blas's story suggest that he has finally found himself, after wandering
through the crystal palace of his various reflections, and that
he no longer needs to investigate his motives and to justify
himself? Richard Bjornson thinks so, contending that "no

matter how much Gil Blas compromises his integrity while accommodating himself to a corrupt society, his noble nature functions as an indestructible kernel of selfhood; as long as he maintains a humble, intellectually honest attitude, his noble character will ultimately be rewarded by an appropriate place in the hierarchy."[17] Such an interpretation seems sound only if one chooses to ignore the intricate reverberations and multiple reflections upon which the novel is built. Associating Gil Blas with an "indestructible kernel of selfhood" amounts to a gross exaggeration, not to say a misreading of the text. As for Gil Blas's intellectual attitude, it is, as we have seen, anything but honest. Bjornson further states that Gil Blas "possesses a sufficiently strong sense of identity to avoid becoming totally corrupted by society."[18] Resting one's analysis on Gil Blas's sense of identity, as Bjornson does, appears very risky in view of the protagonist's protean qualities. It is significant that Bjornson cannot define this "indestructible kernel of selfhood," nor can he present evidence for Gil Blas's integrity and intellectual honesty. As for the nobility of which he speaks, it is based on no objective criteria, but rather on a naive and literal acceptance of the narrator's partiality toward his younger self.[19] Confusing the protagonist's voice with the narrator's, Bjornson inadvertently imitates the narrator's self-indulgence. In the same manner, Gil Blas's "constant need to have a master" reflects as much his lack of identity as any "resignation" to the order of society, since the master represents a figure that he may comfortably imitate at the same time as he frees himself from all responsibility by limiting himself to obeying orders.[20] The im-

[17] Richard Bjornson, *The Picaresque Hero* (Madison: University of Wisconsin Press, 1977), p. 213.

[18] Ibid., p. 214.

[19] The narrator treats young Gil Blas's ignorance with gentle irony to convey that he is tricked because of his innocence, i.e., that he is better than the world around him.

[20] Although I would agree that Gil Blas's need for a master is more than

plication of my analysis is that Gil Blas *exists* only as long as he has a master—that is, someone to imitate.

By the end of the novel, Gil Blas is no longer a servant; he has become his own master, and it is legitimate to wonder whether this circumstance does not account for the impersonal quality of the last part of his memoirs. Since Gil Blas is nothing but the copy of a copy, he can only describe himself by referring to somebody else. Once he has nobody to imitate and to please, he becomes a nobody. In his desire to please, he even forgets at times that Scipio is his servant and not his master: "Afin que Scipion n'eût rien à me reprocher, j'eus la complaisance de continuer le même manège pendant trois semaines" (Book 11, p. 273).*mm* As a consequence, when he becomes his own master, he has to write his memoirs. No longer able to be someone else's reflection, he must find another kind of mirror-play in order to exist, and thus attempts to re-create himself through writing.

The self that appears in the autobiographical account is therefore a copy of an attempted copy of the model available, the "real self."[21] But for the real self, which has never possessed a distinct identity, the autobiographical self has another function. It must project that coherence and identity lacking in the author, and trace the evolution that culminates in the self at the time of writing. This kind of autobiography resembles the falsified archive, the rewritten history of a totalitarian power; and not surprisingly, since it emanates from the author's efforts at totalization. Through writing the individual shapes himself.

---

merely psychological, his universality (his friend Fabrice calls him a "Jack-of-all-trades"), inherited from the picaresque hero, is enhanced by the impossibility of finding a natural destiny or outlet within the social structure of the time.

[21] See the Introduction for an attempt at clarifying this slippery concept of the self in the eighteenth century.

Writing his memoirs may be a disguise or masquerade in which he can change roles at will. Although the disguise will be an idealization in the sense of stylization, it may not always be noble, and in fact is often ignoble and foolish early in this novel. What we see is thus a compromise between the idealization of the protagonist and the creation of the persona of the literary narrator. The movement of signification or copying is once again double. The protagonist and the (philosophical) subject of the narration represent the ideal protagonist and ideal narrator, respectively. Both of these in turn create the duality of the Gil Blas who is writing: he is, on the one hand, the product, embodiment, and imperfect copy of his adventures, like the Quixote we see in the second part of Cervantes's novel; on the other hand, he is, as a writer, the child of his book. In writing, Gil Blas will not be able to dredge up the memory of a true self; he will only be capable of recapitulating his various metamorphoses, skimming the surface of a surface life. Ultimately the narrator can consider his past existence only from the outside, hence the third-person or impersonal quality of the last part of his memoirs.[22]

ROLE-PLAYING is of paramount importance in *Moll Flanders* as well. Moll had not only "several shapes to appear in,"[23] but also several names in the course of her existence. Furthermore, the "penitent" narrator of *Moll Flanders* is still hiding behind an alias as she is writing her memoirs: "It is not to be expected I should set my Name, or the Account of my Family to this Work. . . . It is enough to tell you, that as some of my worst

[22] As René Démoris, who astutely perceived and expressed the continuity between the narrator and the protagonist without confusing them, puts it, "La parole du narrateur, comme celle du héros, est creuse, parce qu'elle n'est pas réaction originale d'un être qui veut apprécier son expérience vécue, mais un effet second du rôle qu'il joue." *Le Roman*, p. 374.

[23] Daniel Defoe, *Moll Flanders*, ed. Edward Kelly (New York: Norton, 1973), p. 185. All subsequent references will be to this edition.

Comrades . . . knew me by the Name of Moll Flanders; so you may give me leave to speak of myself under that Name till I dare own who I have been, as well as who I am" (p. 7). The narrator's attitude is ambivalent from the outset, since she is deliberately exposing herself through the act of writing her life, while simultaneously desiring to conceal her identity. In *Gil Blas*, role-playing reflected the imitative function of the hero; in *Moll Flanders* it expresses the necessity to appear to be what one is not. Gil Blas's memoirs abound in mirrors and reflections; Moll's book focuses on concealment. She constantly emphasizes the need to remain unknown: "I resolv'd therefore, as to the State of my present Circumstances; that it was absolutely Necessary to change my Station, and to make a new Appearance in some other Place where I was not known, and even to pass by another Name if I found Occasion" (p. 61; cf. also pp. 188, 194). This almost pathological fear of being "known" is acute in the part of her memoirs dealing with her husband-hunting, as well as in that which recounts her life as a thief: "One of the greatest Dangers I was now in, was that I was too well known among the Trade" (p. 167).

As a consequence of this necessary concealment, Moll is a much more solitary figure than Gil Blas. Moll blames her circumstances of life on the fact that she is friendless. She maintains that she could not resist seduction by the elder brother because she had nowhere else to go: "with no Friend, no Acquaintance in the whole World, *out of that Town*, and there I could not pretend to Stay; all this terrify'd me to the last Degree . . ." (p. 45; cf. also pp. 83, 101, 221). The concept of isolation is constantly linked to that of hiding in her discourse: "And I had not one Friend to advise with in the Condition I was in, at least not one I durst Trust the Secret of my Circumstances to. . . . Upon these Apprehensions the first thing I did was to go quite out of my Knowledge, and go by another Name" (p. 51; cf. also p. 148). If Moll's solitude is one of the most picaresque aspects of her story, it also accounts for the existence of her memoirs; since she cannot entrust her life to anyone, as she repeatedly points out, her confession requires a book: "... and as I had no Friend in the World to communicate my distress'd Thoughts to, it lay so heavy upon me, that it threw me into Fits and Swoonings several times a-Day" (p. 221). Her book functions as a kind of release in which she can give vent to her long pent-up passions.

Writing is for Moll a way of claiming her existence. By the act of revelation, as well as by what is revealed, she creates herself. Writing is an affirmation of power, a desire to invent as well as to discover herself. Through her "I" she imposes herself as subject, and, since the narrative voice as "I" never enters the text unaccompanied by a "you" or narratee (as Benveniste's remark, quoted in the Introduction, points out), writing allows Moll to display herself while still retaining some secrets. This accounts for the much more active part played by the contrived reader—she does not hesitate to tug at his sleeve at times—in her memoirs than in those of Gil Blas. But Moll (as opposed to Tristram Shandy) cannot accept the implication that she is writing for her own gratification. Hence the difficulty in distinguishing between the "I" of the protagonist and that of the narrator, or "Moll's muddle," as Howard L. Koonce calls this confusion.[24]

On the surface level, the narrator's outlook on her life is that of the Christian reformed sinner: "... the publishing of this Account of my Life is for the Sake of the just Moral of every part of it, and for Instruction, Caution, Warning, and Improvement to every Reader ..." (p. 255). Not unlike Alemán's Guzmán de Alfarache, Moll's stated purpose in writing about herself is not self-glorification, but rather the confession of her

---

[24] Howard L. Koonce, "Moll's Muddle: Defoe's Use of Irony in *Moll Flanders*," in *Twentieth-Century Interpretations of "Moll Flanders*," ed. Robert C. Elliott (Englewood Cliffs, N.J.: Prentice-Hall, 1970), pp. 49-59.

crimes for the moral edification of the reader. This purpose, which bears the stamp of her present prosperity, accounts for the larger amount of moralizing in Moll's discourse than in Gil Blas's. However, even the casual reader of Moll Flanders's memoirs soon realizes that the temporal gap that should exist between the "I" of the criminal protagonist and that of the penitent narrator is not as wide as one might expect in this form. Contrary to what happens in most of Gil Blas's memoirs, in Moll's the act and the content of the narrative event are often impossible to distinguish. Although Ian Watt qualifies this aspect of Defoe's narrative technique as "somewhat primitive,"[25] Defoe's perception—unconscious or not—that a tale of the past is an inseparable compound of past actions and present attitudes constitutes the modernity of *Moll Flanders*, and probably accounts for its continued popularity.

Whereas the narrator's attitude toward the protagonist moves progressively in *Gil Blas* from irony to stigmatizing requisitory to extreme discretion, Moll's strategy is less varied: more systematic, but also more intricate, although it follows the same basic pattern (with a few variations) in those episodes of her life that she develops fully. Her tactic consists in first minimizing her crime or misdeed by pointing to extenuating circumstances, blaming her action on the devil or on some unknown force; then she confesses, accuses herself of wrongdoing, and shows how repulsive her past actions appear to her now. The overall effect is a condemnation of the heroine's circumstances rather than her deeds; hence a certain incoherence that the older Moll does not seem to notice. The episode in which she relates her first theft illustrates how the narrator's twisted mind works. She starts by appealing to the reader's sympathy: "O let none read this part without seriously reflecting on the Circumstances of a desolate State, and how they

[25] Ian Watt, "Defoe as Novelist: *Moll Flanders*," in *Rise of the Novel*, p. 20.

would grapple with meer want of Friends and want of Bread.
... Let 'em remember that a time of Distress is a time of
Dreadful Temptation ..." (p. 149). The tone is that of the
preacher addressing his congregation from the pulpit, rather
than that of the penitent. As if the excuse of "Want" and "Mis-
ery" were not sufficient, Moll then shifts the blame from herself to some mysterious force, which she will later characterize
as the "Devil": "When prompted by I know not what Spirit,
and as it were, doing I did not know what, or why ... but as
the Devil carried me out and laid his Bait for me, so he
brought me to be sure to the place, for I knew not whither I
was going or what I did" (p. 149). The implication is that Moll
is not at all responsible for the theft. The whole passage is
rather confused and repetitious, its key words being
"prompted," "Devil," and "voice," which the narrator endlessly repeats, as if she were still mesmerized. What is striking
in the midst of such confusion is the graphic quality, the details
and clarity, with which she describes the setting of the scene
itself:

> I Pass'd by an Apothecary's Shop in *Leadenhall-street*,
> where I saw lye on a Stool just before the Counter a little
> Bundle wrapt in white Cloth; beyond it stood a Maid
> Servant with her Back to it, looking up towards the top
> of the Shop, where the Apothecary's Apprentice, as I
> suppose, was standing up on the Counter, with his Back
> also to the Door, and a Candle in his Hand, looking and
> reaching up to the upper Shelf for something he wanted,
> so that both were engag'd mighty earnestly, and no Body
> else in the Shop. (p. 149)

All that is left for Moll to do is to pick up the bundle and leave.
Such a passage, locked as it is between confused paragraphs in
which she describes herself as a sleepwalker, has the effect of
undermining the mechanical and fated quality which the nar-

rator is attempting to impose on the circumstances of the theft. Moll's careful description of the layout of the place totally annihilates the suggestion of her lack of premeditation.

The narrator then characteristically proceeds to depict her revulsion at the thought of her crime: "It is impossible to express the Horror of my Soul all the while I did it. . . . The Horror of the Fact was upon my Mind" (p. 150). Moll's act of contrition follows as she pities her victims: "Perhaps, *said* I, it may be some poor Widow like me, that had packed up these Goods to go and sell them for a little Bread for herself and her poor Child" (p. 150). But once again, just as her lack of responsibility is contradicted by her careful description of the scene, Moll's contrition is immediately undercut as she proceeds in the same breath to relate her next theft, which involves the child with the gold necklace. Here again the narrator follows the same pattern, alleging the "dreadful Necessity of [her] Circumstances" (p. 151), the "evil Counsellor within . . . continually prompting [her] to relieve [her]self by the worst means" (ibid.), inducing her to go "she knew not whither, in search of she knew not what." The only innovation here is that although the "Devil" prompts her to kill the child, Moll is able to resist the temptation to murder, limiting herself to the theft of the necklace, as she self-righteously points out. By emphasizing the evil alternative she rejected she attenuates the evil alternative she chose. According to the usual pattern, she pities her victim, who becomes an "innocent creature" and a "little lamb" as she congratulates herself not only for not killing the child, but for teaching the careless parents and maids a lesson: "As I did the poor Child no harm, I only said to myself, I had given the Parents a just Reproof for their Negligence in leaving the poor little Lamb to come home by it self, and it would teach them to take more Care of it another time" (p. 152). The argument is the same (an object lesson to her victims) when she relates the theft of two rings on a window-sill, "laid by some thoughtless Lady, that had more Money than Forecast" (p. 153); or when she deprives the gentleman she has seduced of his gold watch, snuffbox, sword, and periwig: "There is nothing so absurd, so surfeiting, so ridiculous as a Man heated by Wine in his Head, and a wicked Gust in his Inclination together ... picking up a common Woman without regard to what she is, or who she is; whether Sound or rotten, Clean or Unclean" (p. 176). As Moll rambles on she achieves a complete mental reversal of roles from aggressor to victim, as if she were admonishing her own husband for picking up a whore. With a characteristic disregard for logic, she proceeds to pity the gentleman, as if she had totally forgotten her responsibility for his misfortune: "A Gentleman that had no harm in his Design; a Man of Sense, and of a fine Behaviour; a comely handsome Person, a sober solid Countenance, a charming beautiful Face, and everything that cou'd be agreeable" (p. 177). As usual, the narrator seeks to deflect the reader's attention from her own guilt. At times, however, she does it more directly, as when she explains that stealing from a thief is no theft (p. 153).

The above examples illustrate the difficulty of distinguishing between the act and the content of Moll's narrative utterance. Nevertheless, when the narrator wants to convey the problems she has in translating into words what she felt at the time of experience, her voice is as distinct from the protagonist's as that of Gil Blas in his memoirs: "It is impossible to express the Horror of my Soul"; "I cannot express the manner of it" (p. 150); or "he spoke this in so much more moving Terms than it is possible for me to Express" (p. 44). The old Moll also conveys her independence from the protagonist through flashbacks or analepses—"I should go back a little here, to where I left off ..." (p. 46)—or prolepses (p. 102). Sometimes she unquestionably speaks from the vantage-point of her present situation, thus demonstrating the presence in her statements of effects of enunciation, explaining how she would have acted had she possessed the knowledge and experience she now does: "If I had known his Thoughts, and how hard he thought I would be to be gain'd, I might have made my own Terms with him" (p. 21). At times she attempts to elucidate her past behavior and motives, as when she wonders why she did not quit stealing once she had enough "stock," concluding that "as Poverty brought me into the Mire, so Avarice kept me in, till there was no going back" (p. 158).

Philippe Lejeune points out that "one cannot write an autobiography without constructing and communicating a point of view towards oneself."[26] What renders Moll's memoirs so problematic, and why they have puzzled several generations of critics, is that Moll's maneuvers to deflect the reader's attention from her culpability constantly and deviously destroy rather than construct any consistent point of view toward herself. Though particular comments or narrative details in a passage can be identified with various points of view, the incongruities are so noticeable, and the shifts from one point of view to another are so rapid and frequent, that they leave only an impression of instability. Moll's "voice" becomes first polyphony, then cacophony. Blurring matters further is the changing nature of Moll's perspective (a notion that refers to the extent of the narrator's knowledge and understanding of events, as distinguished from the notion of point of view).[27] *Moll Flanders* provides an excellent illustration of the fact that in a personal novel the one who speaks is not necessarily the one who sees, since the perspective can be that of the narrating "I," or of the experiencing "I," or even of a mixture of both. Hence the need to distinguish between point of view and perspective. In many first-person narratives, such as most of *Gil Blas* and

[26] Philippe Lejeune, "Autobiography in the Third Person," *New Literary History* 9 (1977), 20.

[27] Cf. Tzvetan Todorov, *Qu'est-ce que le structuralisme?* (Paris: Seuil, 1968), pp. 64-67; and Genette, *Figures III*, pp. 203-206.

Great Expectations, one may easily distinguish between the retrospective voice of the narrator and his contemporary perspective. This separation is next to impossible in the case of *Moll Flanders*, for many reasons: not simply because the narrator is dishonest and twists her tale, as has often been pointed out, but also because, in spite of her experience, Moll does not see certain aspects of her life in retrospect any more clearly than did the protagonist.

For instance, when she explains in a sentence already quoted that she became a compulsive thief because of her love for money, she is still blind to her real motives. It is clear that both Molls love money and "things"—as demonstrated in the endless lists of stolen items that the narrator remembers—but her main motive for continuing her thieving when she could have retired is her sheer love for her "Trade." This she will not admit, and probably does not even recognize. Although she carefully blames her past crimes rather than herself, as we have seen, what emerges from the narrator's discourse is the real zest with which she tells about her past pranks. She piles up story after story of thefts involving various disguises, on which she dwells with relish, when a few examples would have been sufficient to convey an idea of her corruption. In the same manner as for Rousseau, confessing or writing about a sin functions as a repetition or reenactment of the sin. Moll, unconsciously or not, relives her perilous and seamy life through writing while paying lip service to convention through her moralizing. Although she may be unaware of it, the narrator manifests the pride of the skillful craftsman in her trade, even calling it her "Art" (p. 199). In the following passage she can hardly conceal her glee at the thought of her past exploits: "I could fill up this whole Discourse with the variety of such Adventures which dayly Invention directed to, and which I manag'd with the utmost Dexterity, and always with Success" (p. 188).

Another instance of the narrator's blindness to the complexity of the protagonist, which again does not necessarily indicate her dishonesty, is her interpretation of the Colchester episode at the beginning of her memoirs. According to the pattern delineated above, Moll blames her "crime"—here the loss of her virtue—on circumstances, her isolation in the family, and on the Devil: "But as the Devil is an unwearied Tempter, so he never fails to find opportunity for that Wickedness he invites to" (p. 22). Then she confesses and acknowledges her guilt and proceeds to give her tale a moralizing and instructive twist. "Thus I gave up myself to a readiness of being ruined without the least concern, and am a fair *Memento* to all young Women, whose Vanity prevails over their Virtue" (p. 21). But once more the object lesson is undercut when the narrator lays the blame on the protagonist for the wrong reason. She does not despise young Moll so much for the loss of her virtue as for managing everything wrong: "Nothing was ever so stupid on both Sides. . . . If I had not Capitulated for an immediate Marriage, I might for a Maintenance till Marriage, and might have had *what I would* for he was already Rich to Excess, besides what he had in Expectation; but I seem'd to have wholly *abandon'd all such Thoughts* as these, and was taken up Only with the Pride of my Beauty, and of being belov'd by such a Gentleman" (p. 21). If she had been more clever, whether she had succeeded in inducing the older brother to marry her or not, she could have managed a better deal for herself.

What totally escapes the literal-minded narrator is the sexual nature of her first mistake. The Colchester episode shows that young Moll's attraction to the elder brother is sexual as well as mercenary. Although the narrator does not seem to recognize fully this important aspect of young Moll's nature, it is unmistakably imbedded in her *récit*: "I struggl'd to get away, and yet did it but faintly neither. . . . His Words I must

59

confess fir'd my Blood; all my Spirits flew about my Heart, and put me into Disorder enough" (p. 18); or, ". . . perhaps he found me a little too easie, for God knows I made no Resistance to him while he Only held me in his Arms and Kiss'd me; indeed I was too well pleas'd with it, to resist him much" (p. 19). The elder brother has not offered Moll any money so far, she is merely sexually aroused by his attention. It is only later that he pours gold into her lap, and even then, although the protagonist likes the ring of gold as much as the narrator does, it seems that the elder brother could have obtained her "last favours" gratis: "he went farther with me than Decency permits me to mention, nor had it been it in my Power to have deny'd him at that Moment, had he offer'd much more than he did" (pp. 20-21). This spontaneity and sheer enjoyment of life is what Moll loses when the elder brother abandons her. It is difficult to agree with Robert A. Donovan when he says (in an otherwise perceptive essay) that "Moll's masterstroke of policy is to declare her undying love for the elder brother and her perfect confidence in his intention to make an honest woman of her."[28] This statement could apply to the narrator's discourse, but it is a distortion of the protagonist's real feelings at the time of her affair.

Moll is too innocent in this episode to be able to plan anything; she is merely carried away by her instincts (hence the recurrence of the words "nature" and "natural" throughout). Moreover, she is as confused and unable to understand her motives at the time of the lived event as the narrator, who can-

[28] Robert A. Donovan, *The Shaping Vision: Imagination in the English Novel from Defoe to Dickens* (Ithaca: Cornell University Press, 1966), p. 38. The Colchester episode has received ample critical attention. See also Robert R. Columbus, "Conscious Artistry in *Moll Flanders*," *SEL* 3 (1963), 415-32; and for an insightful analysis of the discrepancies between the values of the narrator and those of the protagonist, Everett Zimmerman, *Defoe and the Novel* (Berkeley and Los Angeles: University of California Press, 1975), pp. 75-106.

not recognize the sexual desires of her former self. Paradoxically, it is much easier in this episode of her memoirs to distinguish between Moll's two voices, probably because old Moll is far too blind to the motives of the protagonist to be able to manipulate her story. She vaguely perceives that what happened in Colchester marks a turning point in her life; and so it does, since it is in Colchester that Moll's values begin to grow muddled. The elder brother's repeated gifts cause love and money to become identified in her mind and she loses her ability to distinguish between the two: "I was more confounded with the Money than I was before with the Love, and began to be so elevated, that I scarce knew the Ground I stood on" (p. 20). When she leaves Colchester the protagonist has already acquired the values that the narrator espouses; she will not change much after this. The narrator's conclusion to the episode emphasizes the alteration in the protagonist: "I had been trick'd once by *that cheat call'd* LOVE, but the Game was over; I was resolv'd now to be Married or Nothing" (p. 48). From now on the narrator will seldom need to reproach the protagonist with her lack of calculation. All feelings not subordinated to a utilitarian purpose will be suppressed; there will be no dichotomy between the narrator's mature and coarse identity and that of the protagonist. After her initiation or corruption, which is also part of the picaresque makeup, Moll's story becomes more problematic; the "I" of the mature narrator is, as often as not, the psychological accomplice of her younger self in spite of its moral pose. After the Colchester episode, which has received so much critical attention, Moll's text rests on a perpetual interchange between discourse and history.

In *Problems of Dostoevsky's Poetics*, Bakhtin defines Dostoevsky's characters as "dialogical heroes":

In Dostoevsky's works the consciousness is never self-sufficient; it always finds itself in an intense relationship with another consciousness. The hero's every experience and his every thought is internally dialogical, polemically colored, filled with opposing forces or, on the other hand, open to inspiration from the outside itself, but in any case does not simply concentrate on its own object. It is accompanied by a constant sideward glance at the other person.[29]

Several aspects of Moll's character correspond to Bakhtin's definition of a "dialogical hero." In an earlier discussion of Gil Blas's "monological" discourse the signifier was limited to equivalence with the signified in a process of imitation and mimesis; yet in the constant play of regression and reference, of multiplied mimesis, any specular "truth" disappears. The signified is no more than a signifier precipitating further regression, in what modern criticism might call a "deconstruction" of the monological. In Moll's discourse the reverse is true: the signified is constantly in excess. In her world things and situations are multifaceted. When her "gentleman draper" flees to France after his bankruptcy, Moll describes herself as being a "Widow bewitched, I had a Husband, and no Husband" (p. 51). She frequently describes herself as "a Whore, and no Whore," or "a Thief, and no Thief." In the same manner, her recurring "as they call'd it" (p. 83), "as we call'd her" (p. 9), "as she call'd herself" (p. 86), suggest the disparity between what something is called and what it really is. In Bakhtin's terms, very few words coincide with themselves and their object. As a consequence, the particularity of Moll's discourse is that words lose their importance as *adequate* representations of signified truth.

Moll's thoughts are indeed "internally dialogical" and "filled with opposing forces." This "dialogization" of Moll's discourse is reinforced by the intermingling of her two voices,

[29] Bakhtin, *Problems of Dostoevsky's Poetics*, p. 26.

but it is also created by the duality of the protagonist's nature. This split is emphasized in the first episode of her memoirs by her attraction to both money and sex. Although she vows to separate money from sentimental matters, her account of her subsequent life features an inextricable mingling of cynicism and sentiment. This is exemplified in a late scene in Virginia, in which Moll presents her new-found son with a gold watch, asking him to kiss it for her sake, and adding for the benefit of the reader, "I did not *indeed tell him* that had I stole it from a Gentlewoman's side, at a Meeting-House in London" (p. 264). Moll is constantly torn between generous and cynical impulses, as her reaction to her "partner's" hanging illustrates: she sincerely pities him for being caught, but cannot help adding that his hanging "was the best News to me that I had heard a great while" (p. 171). This dualism is also evident in her ambiguous attitude toward stealing, which she calls her "Trade," then her "Art," as her skill develops. The examples mentioned above feature Moll at the beginning of her career as a thief, but as her experiences proceed the narrator's emphasis shifts to her skill at disguise, and the crime itself is obliterated in the process. For instance, in the episode in which she dresses as a man, Moll congratulates herself with "the Wisdom of my concealing my Name and Sex from him [her partner], which if he had ever known, I had been undone" (p. 170). The reader is also induced to admire Moll's skill at escape; when about to steal a piece of plate, she is apprehended but manages to prove her innocence on the grounds that she has twenty guineas in her pocket: "So I came off with flying Colours, tho' from an Affair, in which I was at the very brink of Destruction" (p. 212). Her dual nature also expresses itself in the discrepancy between the real terror of being caught and hanged and the delight she takes in her pranks.

Critics have noted Moll's dishonesty with herself and with the reader, or blamed the discrepancies existing in her tale on

Defoe's negligence as an artist.[30] But they have not paid enough attention to the sharp split that divides the protagonist and makes her a "dialogical" heroine long before Dostoevsky's characters.[31] We may say that Moll is often "honestly" dishonest with herself and the reader, but she is never really "sardonic," as Ian Watt calls her.

The third element of Moll's discourse (beside the two voices implicit in a retrospective narrative, and the duality of her character) that contributes to the dialogical nature of the narration lies in her relationship to her narratee—that is, the "other consciousness" Bakhtin mentions in his definition. In his discussion of *The Underground Man*, Bakhtin stresses the importance of the role played by what recent criticism calls the narratee or addressee: "In the first words of the confession the internal polemic with the other person is hidden. But the other person's word is invisibly present, determining the style of the speech from within."[32] In the same manner, in her memoirs, Moll converses with an invisible "other person" distinct from the actual reader. Each word she writes is aimed at that person, who, like her, possesses a traditional sense of morality and shares her horror of crime, but understands that "circumstances" and especially poverty may lead one to thievery. Like the Underground Man, although in a less dialectical manner (since she posits a conniving addressee), Moll's speech is under the influence of the anticipated word of her addressee, who acts upon her style from within. Moll's intense relationship

[30] Particularly Watt, in *Rise of the Novel*.

[31] Donovan (*Shaping Vision*) distinguishes between what he calls "the two heroines of *Moll Flanders*." He is one of the few readers of *Moll Flanders* to have perceived that "what remains as a potentially fruitful organizing principle is the relation between Moll as character and Moll as narrator, is the curiously devious process by which Moll apprehends and organizes the details of her own experience" (p. 36). What Donovan fails to underline is that this duality exists already in the protagonist.

[32] Bakhtin, *Problems of Dostoevsky's Poetics*, p. 191.

with herself is thus complicated by a no less intense dialogical relationship with her narratee. Her numerous references to other thieves as "they" or to gentlefolk as "we" are not inconsistencies on Defoe's part, as Watt would have it,[33] but important marks of enunciation in the narrator's discourse. Through her use of "they," Moll carefully distinguishes herself from the tribe of common thieves; and through her use of "we" she willfully associates herself as well as her narratee with a reputable class of people.

Moll's relationship to the world in which she lives is no less dialogical. Her memoirs rest on a dialectic between the self and the other. In the opening scene of the book young Moll begins by opposing herself to society in her adamant resolution not to serve, but to become a "gentlewoman" in spite of her low birth. Whereas Gil Blas drifts from the start, opening himself to the possibility of any chance meeting, and ready to become anything that "offers" (in Moll's language), Moll appears less malleable. Although what she means by "gentlewoman" is not very clear, she has a definite conception of what she does not want to become: "for I had a thorough Aversion to going to Service, as they call'd it, that is to be a Servant, tho' I was so young" (p. 9). Moll's will to defy her birth amounts to the subversion of a rigid social principle, and accounts for the many disguises in which she appears, as well as the multiple roles she assumes while struggling to survive in defiance of society. As she herself points out, "I took care to make the World take me for something more than I was" (p. 100). Moll's survival in London—where she might meet the shadow of the

---

[33] In Watt, *Rise of the Novel*: "Then a further confusion about the point of view becomes apparent: we notice that to Moll Flanders other pickpockets, and the criminal fraternity in general, are a 'they,' not a 'we.' She speaks as though she were not implicated in the common lot of criminals; or is it perhaps Defoe who has unconsciously dropped into the 'they' he himself would naturally use for them?" (p. 98).

gallows at every turn—indeed depends on her ability to make others take her for what she is not. Her various disguises as a man, a beggar, a wealthy widow, or a maid-servant always prove to be her safest avenue of escape. As she proudly explains, "I took up new Figures, and contriv'd to appear in new Shapes every time I went abroad" (p. 205).

Although Moll routinely complains about her solitude, and expresses her need to confide her secrets, when she has the opportunity to do so, she refrains from revealing herself completely. Her relationships with Jemmy, her "Lancashire husband," and her governess, whom she also calls "Mother," are significant in that respect. The governess is clearly presented as an ally from the start, yet Moll disguises herself from her as she does from her victims: "I told her the strangest Thing in the World had befallen me, and that it had made a Thief of me, even without any design, and so I told her the whole Story of the Tankard" (p. 156). Moll withholds from the governess the information that this is not her first theft, but by means of this partial confession, she learns more about the governess— namely, that the latter is also a thief—than she reveals about herself. The process is the same in her relationship with Jemmy. She actually takes the lead by pretending to reveal more about herself than she actually does. When they first meet they are both taken in by their mutual masquerade, but when they reunite in Newgate Moll dominates Jemmy by preserving her usual prudence: "I told him so much of my Story as I thought was convenient. . . . I told him I far'd the worse for being taken in the Prison for one *Moll Flanders* . . . but that as *he knew well* was none of my Name" (p. 233). Characteristically, at the moment when she plans and actively plots to spend the rest of her life with Jemmy, Moll is still under the compulsion to hide from him. To match Jemmy's "honest Account of his Stock" (p. 243), Moll "gave him an Account of my Stock as faithfully, that is to say of what I had taken to carry with me, for I was resolv'd that what ever should happen, to keep what I had left with my Governess, in Reserve" (p. 244). Later, in Virginia, Moll, conceals her exact relationship with her son by her husband/brother from Jemmy, and tells her son that Jemmy is a friend and not her husband.

Moll's desire to limit and distort what she tells (while insisting on the urge to confide) when she could reasonably reveal herself is another aspect of her dual nature and her need for disguise. It demonstrates her inability to live without masks. Disguise and dissimulation are so central to her personality that the mask finally sticks to the face and becomes inseparable from the self. But what is so fascinating in Moll's memoirs is that her many masks and secrets give the illusion of constituting the center of her personality. It seems that as long as Moll keeps a secret (which assumes the same function as a disguise) she has a core.

Whereas Gil Blas is a servile copy of his environment, Moll sets herself apart in her refusal to submit to a given social hierarchy. Moll's identity is essentially negative in that she not only distinguishes herself from the other (society) in her refusal of a fixed system of signs (the social hierarchy), she also sets herself apart from her past self.[34] So does Gil Blas, although he is constantly overwhelmed by others because he has no self, making it possible to say that he lives by proxy in his many roles.

In Moll's case, disguise and successive rejections of the past self (as it becomes fixed, alien, other) *constitute* the self. The self is secret, unknowable, different from what we see or can surmise from past history. In fact, its core is not a definable essence—the secrets change, the disguises vary—but the tension of this secrecy, of this disguise. As such its core is not solid, but

[34] For an antithetical and stimulating reading of *Moll Flanders*, see Arnold Weinstein's *Fictions of the Self: 1550-1800* (Princeton: Princeton University Press, 1980), pp. 85-100.

always sundered by the same *duplicity* (both doubleness and deceit) that marks Gil Blas's copying. Moll's willingness to give up security in order to satisfy her desires does not prevent her from dissolving behind her many masks, like Gil Blas. Writing for her becomes a masquerade through which she changes roles at will: it allows her to reenact her past selves while rejecting them. For her, writing becomes a critical activity (comparable to her activity as a protagonist), which reenacts the text of her life without surrendering itself to the text. In the same manner that Moll the protagonist gained control over others by manipulating them through indirectness, Moll the writer enjoys the text while separating herself from it, in this remaining faithful to her *non serviam*. If, according to Philippe Lejeune, "the name guarantees the unity of our multiplicity; it federates our complexity of the moment and our changes in time,"[35] then Moll's refusal to give her real name to the text is another sign of her indefinable being.

[35] Philippe Lejeune, "Autobiography in the Third Person," *New Literary History* 9 (1977), 30.

CHAPTER TWO

Pamela, La Vie de Marianne, and
Le Paysan parvenu
Self-Imitation—The Appearance
of Reality

ALTHOUGH *Pamela* begins as an epistolary novel, and con-
tinues as a diary when the heroine becomes Mr. B.'s prisoner, Richardson's first novel presents most of the characteristics of fictive memoirs. In *Pamela* there is no real exchange of
letters such as one finds in *Clarissa, Les Liaisons dangereuses*, or
La Nouvelle Héloïse; the heroine is responsible for over 90 per-
cent of the letters submitted by the editor to the reader. The
apparent difference between *Pamela* and a memoir novel is
that in Richardson's novel the lived event and the narrated
event occur simultaneously. In the prefaces to his works Richardson insists on what is for him the superiority of the epistolary novel over related forms: "All the letters are written while
the hearts of the writers must be supposed to be wholly en-
gaged in their subjects ... so that they abound not only with
critical situations, but with what may be called *instantaneous*
descriptions and reflexions."[1] Richardson later calls this "writing to the moment" in the preface to *Sir Charles Grandison*. It
thus comes as no surprise that he should have looked upon the
temporal gap separating the narrator from the protagonist in

[1] Preface to *Clarissa*, Riverside Edition, ed. George Sherburn (Boston:
Houghton Mifflin, 1962), p. xx.

La Vie de Marianne as the major flaw of Marivaux's novel. Pamela's letters indeed abound with such phrases as "just now, just now!"[2] "But hold!" (p. 191), another example, is followed by the present tense, suggesting the simultaneity of her experience and her recording of it. It is significant in this respect that Pamela's first letter to her parents should be interrupted by Mr. B.'s entrance: "Just now, as I was folding up this letter . . . in comes my young master!" (p. 4). Before marrying Pamela, Mr. B. insists on seeing her letters "because they are your true sentiments *at the time*" (p. 292).

In *Pamela* the letter is not only a means of presenting the story, it is a significant agent in the narrative. The fact that the narrated event is contemporary with the lived event transforms the act of narrating into the event.[3] Pamela is supposedly writing to inform her parents about her life in Mr. B.'s house, but it soon becomes evident that they are not the only targets of her missives. On several occasions Pamela makes a resumé of events she has already written about; she writes her letters, in part, because "it may be some little pleasure to me, perhaps, to read them myself, when I am come to you, to remind me of what I have gone through . . ." (p. 39).[4] Pamela is in essence asking her parents to give her the opportunity of reading the novel within the novel, thus accumulating the roles of character, author, editor, and reader.

[2] *Pamela* (New York: Norton, 1958), p. 177. All subsequent references will be to this edition.

[3] For a discussion of the function of the letter in *Pamela*, see Janet Altman's *Epistolarity: Approaches to a Form* (Columbus: Ohio State University Press, 1982), pp. 104-106.

[4] She expresses the same wish later in the novel: "I will continue my writing still, because, may be, I shall like to read it, when I am with you, to see what dangers I have been enabled to escape" (p. 85). Clarissa also refers to her own writing, particularly in the letters addressed to Anna Howe: "You have often heard me own the advantages I have found from writing down everything of moment that befalls me, and of all I *think*, and of all I *do*, that may be of future use to me" (*Clarissa* [London: Everyman, 1978], vol. 2, p. 128).

According to Jean Rousset, "la lettre est naturellement dirigée vers un destinataire sur lequel elle s'efforce d'agir. On s'explore, on se scrute, mais sous le regard d'autrui. Ainsi s'institue un monologue impur, sur lequel ne cesse de se profiler l'interlocuteur absent."[5] This description of the function of the letter applies to Pamela insofar as she constantly seeks her parents' approval: "Was not I right my dear parents" (p. 14); "I hope my conduct will be approved of by you" (p. 202). In the particular case of *Pamela*, however, what Rousset calls "l'interlocuteur absent" needs to be defined. While her parents function as the actual addressees of Pamela's letters, it is evident that Pamela performs mainly for a larger audience. For instance, the long letter in which she relates how she sorted her clothes into three different "bundles" (p. 78) is addressed to her parents; but the scene itself is performed for the benefit of the admiring Mrs. Jervis. Then we learn that all the time Mr. B. was hidden in the closet, watching Pamela through the keyhole. In spite of Richardson's insistence on "writing to the moment," this letter features the same kind of writing as that found in the memoir novel, in which the distance between the narrated event and the lived event is felt. *Pamela* does not feature as many mirror scenes as *La Vie de Marianne*, yet there is no denying that the heroine is always on display and watching herself being watched, and that she merely reproduces through writing her activity as a character. In this respect the apparent unity of Pamela's "I" is as illusory as the "I" of the memoir novel, since she posits herself as object through her writing.

Richardson's "writing to the moment" is a fiction disguising the multiplicity and duality of the epistolary "I." Elizabeth

---

[5] "The letter is naturally directed toward a recipient, on whom it attempts to act. Self-exploration and self-scrutiny may take place, but under another's gaze. What develops is an impure monologue, against the background of which we continually catch glimpses of the absent addressee." Jean Rousset, *Narcisse romancier* (Paris: José Corti, 1972), p. 115.

Hardwick's description of the letter as "a fabric of surfaces, a mask as well suited to affectation as to the affections"[6] applies particularly well to *Pamela*. Equally appropriate to this novel is William Beatty Warner's analysis of Clarissa's activity as a writer: "by giving a narrative, Clarissa assumes the position of subject in her world; but by elaborating a 'self' she makes herself the object of her own analysis and representation. She becomes the most important object to her own subject. This neatly enhances Clarissa's authority by doubling her presence before the reader."[7]

In spite of Richardson's insistence on Pamela's innocence and purity, and notwithstanding his careful use of interruptions and of the present tense to render the spontaneity of his heroine's recording and motives, the very genre he has chosen is as liable to make her appear a hypocrite as a paragon of virtue.[8] The epistolary nature of the novel perhaps explains why its commentators have been divided into "pamelists" and "antipamelists" for over two centuries. Mr. B.'s statement that Pamela is an "artful young baggage" (p. 22) is as accurate as Mrs. Jervis's testimonial that Pamela is "one of the most virtuous and artless young creatures that ever she knew" (p. 21). We hear two voices in *Pamela*, A. M. Kearny asserts, that of Pamela as character, and that of Pamela as author. The epistolary novel here functions as a memoir novel in which the memoir's temporal gap between narrator and protagonist parallels the letter-writer's split between the self and the self objectified. Kearny's identification of the second voice with Richardson is more debatable, however: "In short, we have a voice

[6] Elizabeth Hardwick, *Seduction and Betrayal: Women and Literature* (New York: Random House, 1974), p. 198.

[7] William Beatty Warner, *Reading "Clarissa": The Struggle of Interpretation* (New Haven: Yale University Press, 1979), p. 89.

[8] For a discussion of ambiguity in *Pamela*, see Terry Eagleton's *The Rape of Clarissa* (Oxford: Basil Blackwell, 1982), pp. 30-37.

which is recognizably Pamela's own, and a commentary which is often palpably not . . . but Richardson's own authorial one which he expresses through her."[9] There is no denying that Richardson's voice can be detected in this first unpolished novel,[10] yet it seems that Bakhtin's assumption about the independence of the hero holds true in the case of Pamela. If Richardson's voice can be heard, it must be distinguished from the heroine's several voices.

Pamela's writing of letters constitutes the main action of the novel; at the level of the lived event very little happens. The heroine's first and only act occurs in the middle of the book, when Mr. B. asks her (through writing) to come back to him, thus provoking Pamela's first real dilemma ("Should I go back, or should I not?" p. 264). As if to parallel Pamela's logorrhea the action of the novel is mainly verbal. Each scene follows the same pattern of passionate argument between Pamela and Mr. B., but Pamela always wins so long as their jousts remain on the verbal level, and whenever Mr. B. attempts to translate his words into actions, she is saved by her "lucky knack of falling into fits" (p. 62). In life as well as in her letters Pamela is a conscious user of language. In her endless verbal contests with Mr. B. she insists on the strict connection that should exist between words and actions, as she takes Mr. B.'s uncivil apostrophes to be the explicit proof of his impure intentions: "I see, my dear parents, that when a person will do wicked things, it is no wonder that he will speak wicked words" (p. 35). She similarly justifies her pert attitude to Mr. B. as the result of his own improper conduct: "If I have been

---

[9] A. M. Kearney, "Richardson's *Pamela*: The Aesthetic Case," in *Twentieth-Century Interpretations of "Pamela,"* ed. R. Cowler (Englewood Cliffs, N.J.: Prentice-Hall, 1969), p. 79.

[10] *Pamela* is regarded by most critics as a prelude to Richardson's major works, or as Eagleton puts it, a "pre-run" or "cartoon version" of *Clarissa* (*Rape of Clarissa*, p. 37).

a sauce-box, and a bold-face, and a pert, and a creature, as he calls me, have I not had reason? Do you think I should ever have forgot *myself*, if he had not forgot to act as my *master?*" (p. 35).

What also characterizes Pamela's use of language is her systematic refusal of the figurative meaning of words. When accused of having robbed Mr. B. (that is, of his heart), she claims to be "ignorant of his meaning" (p. 55) and asks to be sent to jail if he can prove it. Mr. B. is thus constantly defeated by Pamela's insistence on calling attention to what he has said rather than to what he means. She uses a similar argument when she defends herself against the accusation of having written love letters to Parson Williams: "Well, sir, said I, that is your comment; but it does not appear so in the text" (p. 241). By constantly defeating Mr. B. through her literal faith in language Pamela shows him that she is a better user of signs than he is.

Whereas language is a sham in *Gil Blas* and inadequate in *Moll Flanders*, in *Pamela* the subject of the enunciation is being both created and judged through language. Even before he sees her letters, Mr. B. has to respect Pamela because of her linguistic abilities. Indeed, the novel revolves around Pamela's awareness of the different meanings that key words such as honor have for her and for Mr. B.: "O, good sir! I too much apprehend that *your* notion of honour and *mine* are very different from one another" (p. 143). She proceeds to tell him that as long as his conception of the word honor differs from hers—namely, family honor as opposed to personal honor— she may not give him leave to see her. Pamela also pursues her linguistic bickerings with her Cerberus, Mrs. Jewkes: "I shall not, at this time, dispute with you about the words *ruin* and *honourable*: for I find we have quite different notions of both ..." (p. 141).

The dichotomy between Pamela's acute linguistic consciousness and her repeated professions of artlessness and innocence is, of course, problematic. She recognizes this ambiguity and justifies herself on several occasions: "Alas! for me, what a fate is mine, to be thus thought artful, and forward, and ungraceful; when all I intended was to preserve my innocence" (p. 172). The ambiguity resides in what can be called the doubleness of Pamela's discourse. Although she takes refuge behind the literal meaning of words, her speech (like her letters) has several recipients who elicit it from within. In her linguistic quarrels, Mr. B. or Mrs. Jewkes are her actual interlocutors, but beyond them she addresses a larger audience composed of herself and of what can appropriately be called the world. Bakhtin's assertion that "every word in a dialogue speech is directed toward its object but at the same time reacts intensely to the word of the other person, answering it and anticipating it"[11] is verified in the case of Pamela; what is special for Pamela is that her "word" passes over the "other person's word" to reach the metalinguistic audience. Pamela creates herself through her speech as well as through her letters.

If we admit that there are two kinds of communication at work in *Pamela*, we can understand why she appears "innocent" and "artless" to some, and an "equivocator" to others. Each of Pamela's statements is endowed with that doubleness: at one level, each word she utters, each dress she wears (as will be shown below), each letter she writes is a statement in which the signifier is adequate to the signified. At another level, each time she makes a statement, she displays herself as a good speaker, a good user of signs (clothes), a good writer. What matters at that level is not the actual communication with the other person, but her self-consciousness of being watched and admired, her histrionic triumph as a maker and user of signs.

If clothing plays an important part in *Gil Blas* and *Moll Flanders*, it is also paramount in *Pamela*, but its function and

[11] Bakhtin, *Problems of Dostoevsky's Poetics*, p. 163.

ultimate meaning are entirely different. Moll uses clothes "to make the world take [her] for something more than she is," whereas Pamela, on the contrary, repeatedly insists on wearing clothes corresponding to her social situation. When she decides to go back to her parents she sews a dress "suitable to my condition . . . that all my fellow-servants might see I knew how to suit myself to the state I was returning to" (p. 52). In the novels examined in the preceding chapter, dress and discourse were endowed with their independent truth; if he wore a gentleman's costume Gil Blas became a gentleman. In *Pamela*, on the other hand, there is meaningful depth behind the various costumes used by the heroine; although clothes are the sign of a particular social status, they do not create it but merely confirm it.

Pamela's obsession with clothing, and with wearing clothes that will most closely fit her social circumstances, is most clearly illustrated when she divides her outfits into three separate "bundles" (p. 76) corresponding to three different social positions. The first bundle is made up of the dresses given to her by her late mistress: "But, since I am to be turned away, you know, I cannot wear them at my poor father's" (p. 78). In the second bundle she puts those offered by Mr. B. for a price that she is not willing to pay: "Thou *second wicked* bundle" (ibid.). The third is composed of the garments she has made as the emblem of her condition: "My dear third bundle, I will hug thee to my bosom" (p. 79). The circumstantiality with which she describes each bundle, and the affection with which she clings to the third one, may be attributable to her feeling of being *déclassée*.[12] She expresses this feeling in her first letter

[12] For an interesting analysis of the clothes motif in *Pamela* see Carey McIntosh's "Pamela's Clothes," *ELH* 35 (1968), 75-83. See also Patricia Meyer Spacks's excellent chapter on *Pamela* in *Imagining a Self: Autobiography and Novel in Eighteenth-Century England* (Cambridge: Harvard University Press, 1976), pp. 216-18. She also insists on the importance of lan-

to her parents: "As my lady's goodness had . . . qualified [me] above my degree, it was not every family that could have found a place that your poor Pamela was fit for" (p. 3; cf. also pp. 6, 7, 74). The death of Pamela's mistress, who had raised her "above her degree," makes her status in the well-structured household of Mr. B. ambiguous.[13] Pamela is the only character at Mr. B.'s Hall (that microcosm of society) whose social status is not clearly defined. The novel thus turns on the heroine's efforts to find her proper place in a rigid social structure. Seen from this angle, the novel's issue is not so much moral (whether Pamela will be able to protect her virtue) as social (whether she will find her place in society). As Robert A. Donovan puts it, "*Pamela* is about morality only in the way that *Robinson Crusoe* is about an island."[14]

The other function of clothes in *Pamela*, as in *Clarissa*, is sexual. When she is not writing, Pamela spends most of her time dressing or undressing; and this quality of the novel, as a drawn-out striptease, has been noted by most of its commentators. But more interesting is the relationship existing in Pamela's mind between clothing as a sign, as language, and its sexual role. By a traditional metonymy she transforms her virtue itself into an ornament or garment as she refuses Mr. B.'s various gifts: "To lose the best jewel, my virtue, would be poorly recompensed by those you propose to give me" (p. 199). The origin of the clash between Mr. B. and Pamela arises from

---

guage and its manipulation in Richardson's novel, pp. 210-14. In *A Natural Passion: A Study of the Novels of Samuel Richardson* (Oxford: Clarendon, 1974), p. 41, Margaret Doody suggests that Pamela's insistence on clothes is symbolic of country innocence and beauty.

[13] In "The Problem of *Pamela*, or Virtue Unrewarded," *SEL* 3 (1963), p. 383, Robert A. Donovan correctly states that "one of the most striking characteristics of the world represented in *Pamela* is the tightness and clarity of its social structure"—a rigidity all the more striking when compared to the fluidity of society in *Gil Blas, Moll Flanders*, or even in *Le Paysan parvenu*.

[14] Ibid., p. 379.

the fact that they do not share the same social values. For Mr. B. virtue in a servant is an anomaly, whereas Pamela is intent on his recognizing the importance of her virtue as well as on his respecting it. In attaching so much importance to her virtue Pamela unconsciously espouses Mr. B.'s aristocratic code and aspires to a higher station than the one she advertises by ostentatiously wearing her common dress. She is also well aware that the impact of her "common garb" is not merely social: "I looked about me in the glass, as proud as anything—To say truth, I never liked myself so well in my life" (p. 51). Mr. B. himself is conscious of the social as well as sexual impact of clothing, when he parades in front of Pamela in his court outfit: "How are these clothes made? Do they fit me?" (p. 65). Although Pamela is impressed by Mr. B.'s stately appearance— "his waistcoat stood on end with silver lace, and he looked very grand" (p. 65)—she is mainly struck by the disparity between his appearance and his actions: "But what he did last [his unsuccessful attempt to assault her], has made me very serious, and I could make him no compliments" (p. 65).

Pamela here insists again on the equivalence that should exist between sign and meaning. Mr. B.'s costume corresponds to his station in life but it clashes with his attitude toward her. Pamela's strategy to defend her virtue consists in demonstrating to Mr. B. that his attempts to violate her body are also violations of his own social code: "Well may I forget that I am your servant, when you forget what belongs to a master" (p. 16). And she goes on to explain that by "lessening the distance" which should exist between them he has also done her "the greatest harm in the world: You have taught me to forget myself and what belongs to me . . . by demeaning yourself, to be so free to a poor servant" (p. 17). By her attitude as well as by her manner, dress and speech, Pamela shows Mr. B. that she is a better user of signs, of the social code, than he is.

This preoccupation with finding and remaining in one's

78

place, with properly playing one's part, is a theme that runs through the novel, climaxing in the famous scene of confrontation with Lady Davers. Pamela triumphs over Lady Davers by demonstrating that she is more aware of her social position than the arrogant lady is: "If you would have me keep my distance, you will not forget your own degree.... If you, madam, said I, lessen the distance yourself, you will descend to my level, and make an equality, which I don't presume to think of; for I can't descend lower than I am—at least in your ladyship's esteem!" (p. 404). Pamela's insistence on the necessity of knowing one's place (cf. pp. 29-30, 36, 85) and keeping one's distance may be interpreted as an attempt on her part to find her own space (both physical and social) in a house where she has no definite status and is constantly spied upon. Mr. B.'s repeated advances thus appear as intrusions on Pamela's privacy, which explains the importance of her "closet," the only room in the house for which she has a key ("So I took refuge in my closet, and had recourse to pen and ink, for my amusement, and to divert my anxiety of mind," p. 367).[15] She expresses the role of pen and ink in an earlier episode: "My pen and ink (in my now doubly-secured closet) are all I have to employ myself with ..." (p. 178). In light of these two sentences, it appears that the only space that Pamela can occupy in Mr. B.'s world is the space which she creates in her writing.[16] Pamela uses both her closet and her letters as refuges against sexual outrage.

Writing as an activity within the text is, of course, inherent to the genre of *Pamela* as an epistolary novel, but very few let-

[15] Robert Folkenflik, in "A Room of Pamela's Own," *ELH* 39 (1972), 585-96, and Ian Watt in *Rise of the Novel*, pp. 188-89, stress the importance of the closet in *Pamela*.

[16] For a discussion of the function of letters in the eighteenth century see Ruth Perry, *Women, Letters, and the Novel* (New York: AMS Press, 1980), and Janet Todd's chapter on *Clarissa* in *Women's Friendship in Literature* (New York: Columbia University Press, 1980), pp. 9-68.

ter-writers are as self-conscious about their activity as Pamela. The heroine acknowledges the importance of her writing early in the novel, when she asks her parents to save her letters so that she may read them when she comes home. Even before her captivity, Pamela insists that she "loves writing" (p. 10).[17] She is indeed an inveterate letter-writer—"a mighty letter-writer," in Mr. B.'s words. Not satisfied with writing letters, she also copies most of the letters she sends or receives. As has been pointed out before, this obsessive urge to turn life into a copy, a text, makes writing in her novel a literal substitute for action.

The function of Pamela's writing in the novel is manifold. It serves not only as a refuge for the protagonist, but is also generally recognized as significant by the other characters. Everybody who has read her prose seems compelled to commend her style: her parents (p. 9), Mr. Peters, the minister (p. 139), Lady Davers herself at the end of the novel, and of course Mr. B. The impact of Pamela's writing is so strong that it actually affects the course of the novel. Squire B. immediately perceives Pamela's activity as a potential threat to his design: "This girl is always scribbling; I think she may be better employed" (p. 15). Once a prisoner, Pamela is characteristically denied pen and ink on Mr. B.'s orders. The correlation between Pamela's writing and her virtue is emphasized early in the novel,[18] when Mr. B. orders Mrs. Jervis "to bid [her] not pass so much time in writing" (p. 20). It is further underlined

[17] It must be noticed that most of Richardson's main characters share their creator's love of writing. Clarissa insists on her "passion for scribbling," and describes Lovelace as "a great writer" at the beginning of *Clarissa*.

[18] In *Clarissa*, Mrs. Harlow perceives her daughter's letter-writing as a potential threat to her virtue, and advises her to read rather than write. Lovelace's desire to interfere with the correspondence between Anna and Clarissa parallels Mr. B.'s attempts to prevent Pamela from writing. Conversely, Lovelace's first step in his seduction of Clarissa will consist in inducing her to write to him, as does Valmont in the case of Mme. de Tourvel.

when after an unsuccessful attempt to rape her, he steals or violates her letters as a substitute for her body. Later in the novel, Pamela's voluntary surrendering of her journal can also be viewed as a symbolic surrendering of herself before she marries Mr. B.

Squire B.'s increasing admiration for Pamela's style and talent as a writer transforms him from a rapist into a lover: "I have seen more of your letters than you imagine, and am quite overcome with your charming manner of writing; . . . and all put together, makes me, as I tell you, love you to extravagance" (p. 83). Her writing later turns him from a lover into a husband, as he tells his friends that the beauties of Pamela's person "just attracted my admiration and made me her lover; but they were the beauties of her mind, that made me her husband" (p. 380). After his conquest of Pamela, Mr. B., no longer threatened by her writing, even encourages her to pursue her activity, while Pamela, on the contrary, is quite willing to give up writing, signifying thereby that Mr. B.'s recognition and acceptance of her renders the space created by her letters no longer necessary.

The function of the heroine's writing is not merely existential (that is, she does not simply create herself and her place in society through this activity),[19] her writing becomes as vital for others as it has been for her by the end of the novel: "I enjoin you, Pamela, to continue your relation, as you have opportunity; and though your father be here, write to your mother, that this wondrous *story* be perfect, and we your friends, may *read* and *admire* you more and more" (p. 317, my emphasis). Mr. B. has been contaminated by Pamela's urge to turn life into a text. Technically the presence of Pamela's father renders a letter to her mother unnecessary, since he could give her an oral account of their daughter's good fortune upon his return.

[19] For a useful discussion of the existential dimension of writing in *Clarissa*, see Warner, *Reading "Clarissa."*

By demanding a letter, Mr. B. is implying that what will give their happy reunion its reality is its being written down; the letter will also give him the opportunity to live it twice. [This attitude is reminiscent of Fielding's interpretation of Colley Cibber's *Apology*.[20] According to Fielding, Cibber only lived his life so that he could write it down, thus making a spectacle of himself through his writing as he did on stage.] At the same time Mr. B. expresses his surrender to the power of Pamela as writer. Earlier in the novel he had accused her of making him a character in her "plot":[21]

> I long to see the particulars of your plot . . . and as I have furnished you with the subject, I have a title to see the fruits of your pen.—Besides, said he, there is such a pretty air of romance, as you relate them in *your* plots, and *my* plots, that I shall be better directed in what manner to wind up the catastrophe of the pretty novel. (p. 242).

The difference between the two statements illuminates the influence of Pamela's writing on Mr. B. At first he still assumes that his reading of Pamela's journal will give him power over her; that the "catastrophe" of what he calls "the pretty novel" depends on his good will, that is, on his decision to marry her or not; in the later statement, however, Mr. B. recognizes Pamela's ultimate control as author. What he also acknowledges is the importance of Pamela's public ("we your friends, may read and admire you more and more").

All of Richardson's novels hinge on his characters' awareness of public opinion. Whatever their social circumstances,

[20] Henry Fielding, *Joseph Andrews* (New York: Signet Classics, 1960), p. 20.

[21] In *Clarissa*, it is Lovelace who is constantly referred to as "a great plotter" by the other characters, and by the author himself in his preface to the novel. For a useful discussion of Lovelace as novelist within *Clarissa*, see Tony Tanner's *Adultery in the Novel* (Baltimore: The Johns Hopkins University Press, 1979), pp. 105 and following.

life is public for them; the individuals' actions are carried out in full view of, and are conditioned by, society. The conflict between Mr. B. and Pamela is complicated by the fact that the demands of public opinion are different for each of them, as Pamela makes clear: "your honour is to destroy mine" (pp. 218-19). Mr. B. obviously runs fewer risks of incurring his neighbors' disapproval by abducting Pamela than by marrying her, as Sir Simon's reaction to Pamela's incarceration demonstrates: "Why, what is all this, my dear, but that our neighbour has a mind to his mother's waiting-maid! And if he takes care she wants for nothing, I don't see any great injury will be done her. He hurts no *family* by this" (p. 138).

The metaphor of the trial recurs in many eighteenth-century novels, conveying the importance of public opinion.[22] Mr. B. (who is also a justice of the peace) sets himself up as Pamela's judge on several occasions, using his upper servants Mrs. Jervis and Mr. Longman, and later the ominous Mrs. Jewkes (p. 194), as his witnesses against Pamela: "Well, said my master, this is a little specimen of what I told you, Longman. You see there's a spirit you did not expect. . . . Come, Pamela, give another specimen, I desire you, to Longman" (p. 72). Later, what renders Squire B.'s decision to marry Pamela particularly excruciating is his apprehension of how she will be received by the neighboring gentry: "What must we do about the world, and the world's censure?" (p. 229). Consequently, his first act after marrying her is to invite his neighbors to meet Pamela and communicate their approval. Because of his sex and his well-defined social status, Mr. B. enjoys more freedom than Pamela, yet for him too, the self needs, and exists in, the sight and approval of others. Predictably Pamela uses his concern for public opinion as a weapon against his advances: "What, sir, would the world say, were you to marry your harlot?" (p. 201).

---

[22] There are also several trial scenes in *Moll Flanders, La Vie de Marianne*, and *Le Paysan parvenu*.

The verdict of public opinion is, of course, more crucial for a character who, like Pamela, must find her proper place in society, which is why Pamela demands not only that Mr. B. refrain from violating her virtue, but that he recognize its importance. Virtue, like the self, must be acknowledged in order to be real. Her actions are governed by two contrasting motives: on the one hand, the desire to assert herself while retaining her integrity against the expectations of the world and in opposition to it (cf. Sir Simon's comment); and on the other, the need for public approval. Her obsession with wearing the right kind of clothing thus appears endowed with a double meaning: the desire to fit her station, but also and above all, the need to appear to fit her station before a public ("that all my fellow-servants might *see* I knew how to suit myself to the state I was returning to," p. 52). When she is offered Mr. B.'s carriage to go home, Pamela's first reaction is to decline it, but on second thought she realizes that ". . . this will *look* too great for me, yet it will *shew* as if I was not turned away quite in disgrace" (p. 80). To "see," to "show," and to "look" (in all its meanings) are indeed key words in Pamela's vocabulary. "In what light must I appear to the world" (p. 247), together with the preservation of her virtue, are her main, and of course related, preoccupations. As the novel progresses it becomes increasingly clear that for Pamela life is largely a performance before audience. As she repeatedly points out, Mr. B. "may be ashamed by *his* part; I not of *mine*" (p. 15). Mr. B. can marry her because she "knows how to perform a part there, as well as in the other diversions" (p. 276). In her confrontation with Lady Davers she is accused of playing a role: "I'll warrant my little dear has topped her part, and paraded it like any real wife. . . . Survey thyself, and come back to me, that I may see how finely thou can'st act the theatrical part given thee!" (p. 409).

Given the impact of public opinion in Richardson's world,

it comes as no surprise that theatrical references should pervade the novel, and that all the characters should be aware of playing some kind of part. What renders Pamela's role particularly interesting is that she acts as both author and performer through her writing, and her letters are a privileged means to act before her public. Once she knows that her letters have a growing public (first her parents, to whom they are presumably addressed, then Mr. B., and later Lady Davers and the neighbors), her sense of pride as author protects her virtue as she enlarges her sense of self through writing and being read. Through her letters Pamela becomes the author of herself under the gaze of her public, as she watches herself being watched. In spite of her reiterated protests that "what one writes to one's father and mother, is not for everybody to see" (p. 239),[23] Pamela revels in watching Mr. B. read her letters: He "seemed so moved, that he turned away his face from me, . . . and I began not so much to repent at his seeing this mournful part of my story" (p. 252). This "mournful part of [her] story" is nothing less than Pamela's relation of her temptation to commit suicide, and most interestingly, her imagining people's reaction to her death, so that the actual reader of the novel reads about an "author" watching a character in the novel read one of the most narcissistic scenes ever written in literature:

> And when they see the dead corpse of the unhappy Pamela dragged out of these dewy banks, and lying breathless at their feet, they will find that remorse so soften their obdurate heart, which now has no place there!—And my master, my angry master, will then forget his resentments, and say, O, this is the unhappy Pamela! that I have so carelessly persecuted and destroyed! Now do I see she preferred her honesty to her life, will he say, and

[23] Cf. also p. 240, "remember only, that they were not written for your sight."

is no hypocrite, nor deceiver; but really was the innocent creature she pretended to be! . . . And the young men and maidens all around my dear father will pity poor Pamela! But, O! I hope I shall not be the subject of their ballads and elegies; but that my memory, for the sake of my dear father and mother, may quickly slide into oblivion. (pp. 180-81)

It is of course not infrequent in literature—or in "real" life—that one should compose one's own eulogy; as far as Pamela is concerned, this is one of the most illuminating passages of the book. Not only does it encapsulate the novel—it is another *mise en abyme* of Pamela's activity—but it also throws light on Pamela's character and priorities. The movement of the passage shifts from the "world's" reaction to her death, to Mr. B., and back to the world—the larger audience. It corroborates what has already been suggested at the beginning of this study: Pamela's aim is not so much to marry Mr. B. at all costs (except that of her virtue), but rather to find her place and space in society, to create her own importance. The conclusion, which undermines in one simple sentence the preceding high-flown elegy, is representative of Pamela's discourse and actions throughout, as she expresses the desire to sink into oblivion after making her public lavish a page of praises over her dead body. The fact that her parents' grief is not even alluded to is another proof that they are only the technical recipients of her letters. In this passage Pamela is wearing several masks simultaneously: she is again actor and director as she gives Mr. B. his cue ("Now do I see . . . but really was the innocent creature she pretended to be!"). The word *pretended* is particularly pertinent here; Pamela evidently means "she said she was," but given the context in which it is used, its meaning of pretense cannot escape the extradiegetic reader of the novel. What Pamela is offering here and everywhere in her text is a highly

86

manipulated version of herself and of appearances; only through it can her reality be recognized. As she joins the crowd to watch the dead corpse of "the unhappy Pamela," her spectator status is exactly the same as the one she has occupied all along, objectifying herself to watch herself being watched and approved.

Although *Pamela* features a quest for literalness and exact correspondence between sign and meaning, as exemplified by the heroine's use of clothing and language—and clothing considered *as* language—the unity of Pamela's "I" is only apparent; it designates a self that she is striving to create. To the two recipients of her letters and actions—the actual addressee and the metalinguistic addressee—correspond Pamela's two "I's."

WHEREAS *Pamela* is an epistolary novel that functions as a memoir novel, *La Vie de Marianne* owes as much to the epistolary genre (the eleven parts that compose the novel may be taken as letters addressed by Marianne to her lady friend) as to fictive memoirs (Marianne herself uses the word: "le titre que je donne à mes Mémoires . . .")[24] Marivaux's novel thus combines the advantages inherent to the two forms: Marianne may indulge in the familiarity of epistolary language and achieve the "writing to the moment" effect so dear to Richardson. Through recurrent imperative and present tenses ("vous voulez que j'écrive mon histoire. . . . N'oubliez pas que vous m'avez promis . . ." p. 9)[a] the recipient of Marianne's letters is at least as present as those of Pamela's.[25] The "you" to whom the story is told is in fact more central to Marivaux's novel than to Richardson's, as we shall see. At the same time Marianne

[24] Marivaux, *La Vie de Marianne*, ed. Frédéric Deloffre (Paris: Garnier, 1963), p. 63. All subsequent references will be to this edition.

[25] For a discussion of the role of the reader in *La Vie de Marianne*, see Altman's *Epistolarity* (pp. 90-99) as well as the second chapter of her study, in which she emphasizes the conjunction in French epistolary fiction of the themes of *confiance* and *confidence*.

takes the stand of the memorialist ("je conte mon histoire," p. 63); she tells her past story from the perspective of her present condition. Contrary to Pamela, Marianne the narrator is separated from the protagonist by a gap of many years; the narrator's outlook spans a larger portion of the protagonist's life. Moreover, the events of her life are narrated not only from the perspective of facts past, but also from that of events yet to come, as exemplified by the frequent use of the future and related tenses ("Que de folies je vais bientôt vous dire . . ." p. 21).[b]

The intricate relationship between the protagonist and the narrator of *La Vie de Marianne* constitutes one of the most fascinating aspects of Marivaux's novel. Marianne's discourse is characterized by a constant shuttling back and forth between the rather elastic past (not limited to one precise moment) of the memorialist and the present of the letter-writer. The narrator's running commentary on the protagonist's actions was not used so extensively before Marivaux, and it represents one of his main contributions to the French first-person novel. It comes as no surprise that Marivaux should have been the first explorer of this possibility, since it suited so perfectly the constant preoccupation of all his writing (journalistic, theatrical, as well as novelistic): the knowledge of the self. What marks Marivaux's characters is their momentary confusion, or even blindness, at the time of action. By positing a narrator inclined to introspection, he unites the lucidity of retrospection to the vividness of action, a combination impossible in theater. In a well-known essay, Jean Rousset throws light on the gap between these two paramount aspects of Marivaux's world: what is felt as opposed to what is known by his characters.[26] Rousset shows that what he calls "le double registre" is represented in Marivaux's theater by two types of characters: those who act, and are led by instinct, and their servants who watch and can

[26] Jean Rousset, "Marivaux ou la structure du double registre," *Studi Francesi* 1 (1957), 58-63.

better elucidate their masters' behavior. He explains that in Marivaux's fictive works, this "double registre" is still represented, but is united in a character who is both actor and spectator. This distinction allows Rousset, in a more recent essay, to insist on Marianne's "regard lointain et rectificateur," and "la distance établie par la narratrice entre le moment où elle écrit et celui où elle vivait ses émotions."[27]

The metaphor of the *regard* is an apt one to describe the activity of any Marivaldian character; the French word suggests a nexus of concepts that include look, outlook, and observation, both vision and revision, a diversity structurally important in Marivaux's work. What characterizes Marianne the narrator is the variety of her outlooks. Sometimes, especially at the beginning of her story, her vision is indeed distant as she relates the bare facts of her circumstances: "je restai dans cet état un bon quart d'heure, toujours criant, sans pouvoir me débarrasser" (p. 10).[c] Her discourse becomes more personal when she wants to convey the sense that only after time can one record and understand what one has experienced: "Tout ce que je vous dis là, je ne l'aurais point exprimé, mais je le sentais" (p. 40; cf. also p. 394).[d] At times the narrator attempts to give deeper insight into the heroine's consciousness: "A présent que j'y pense, je crois que je ne consultais que pour gagner du temps" (p. 39);[e] or to point out the young girl's blindness to her own motives: "Et ce qui est plaisant, c'est que je trouvais la réparation fort bonne, et que je la recevais de la meilleure foi du monde, sans m'apercevoir qu'elle n'était qu'une répétition de la faute" (p. 75).[f] All along, the narrator's discourse is punctuated by general commentaries on her past experience. Sentences like: "Apparemment que l'amour, la

---

[27] Marianne's "distant and rectifying perspective"; "the distance the narrator preserves between her moment of writing and the moment at which she actually experienced the emotions she describes." Jean Rousset, *Narcisse romancier*, pp. 104, 131.

première fois qu'on en prend, commence avec cette bonne foi-
là, et peut-être que la douceur d'aimer interrompt le soin
d'être aimable" (p. 63), or "c'est que, dans la vie, nous sommes
plus jaloux de la considération des autres que de leur estime"
(p. 87),[g] could easily find a place alongside La Rochefoucauld's
Maximes. Old Marianne also makes frequent comments on her
own discourse, particularly at the beginning and end of each
"letter": "Ma réflexion n'est pas si mal placée, je l'ai faite sim-
plement un peu plus longue que je ne le croyais" (p. 87).[h] As
opposed to the maxims, such comments bear on the form and
style of her memoirs rather than on their content.

In all these instances in which the narrator casts an indul-
gent glance upon her past self, attempts to elucidate her past
behavior by exposing the heroine's motives, or aphoristically
philosophizes, the position of the narrator may vary, but her
voice is quite distinct from that of the heroine. Very often,
however, the narrator's perspective is far more problematic,
and the two "registers" tend to mingle. This is the case in the
important episode in which the narrator relates Marianne's
passage from innocence to experience in her relationship with
M. de Climal.[28] The narrator starts by giving instances of Marianne's innocence in her dialogue with Climal: "Eh! vous par-
lez donc de coeur, chère enfant, et le vôtre, si je vous le de-
mandais, me le donneriez-vous? Hélas vous le méritez bien,
lui dis-je naïvement" (p. 37).[i] She then immediately depicts
Marianne's loss of naiveté in a typically Marivaldian fashion:
"Je vis dans ses yeux quelque chose de si ardent que ce fut
comme un coup de lumière pour moi ... tout d'un coup les
regards de M. de Climal me parurent d'une espèce suspecte"

---

[28] This episode has received close critical scrutiny, for instance in Henri
Coulet's *Marivaux romancier* (Paris: Armand Colin, 1975) and Ronald C.
Rosbottom's *Marivaux's Novels: Theme and Function in Early Eighteenth-
Century Narrative* (Rutherford, N.J.: Fairleigh Dickinson University Press,
1974).

(p. 37).[j] After having described the heroine's initiation, the narrator throws some light on what must be called Marianne's casuistry. Although she has discovered that Climal is a libidinous hypocrite, she rationalizes in order to accept the dress that her protector intends to buy for her; in spite of the "coup de lumière," the heroine (or is the narrator speaking?) claims that "je doutais encore de ce qu'il avait dans l'âme, et supposé qu'il n'eût que de l'amitié, c'était donc une amitié extrême, qui méritait assurément le sacrifice de toute ma fierté. Ainsi j'acceptai l'offre de l'habit à tout hasard" (p. 38).[k] It seems that here the narrator espouses the heroine's self-mystification; the use of the present tense justifies this interpretation: "je crois que j'aurais refusé si j'avais été bien convaincue qu'il avait de l'amour pour moi" (p. 38).[l] Although she uncovers the heroine's secret motives, thereby underlining her honesty as a narrator, the mature Marianne indirectly excuses the protagonist, making it difficult to speak of a "distant outlook."

Yet the narrator regains some distance when she relates how M. de Climal insists on buying "du linge trop distingué," as she exposes the protagonist's rationalization for accepting the disreputable gift:

> Je consultais donc en moi-même ce que j'avais à faire; et à présent que j'y pense, je crois que je ne consultais que pour gagner du temps: j'assemblais je ne sais combien de réflexions dans mon esprit; je me taillais de la besogne, afin que, dans la confusion de mes pensées, j'eusse plus de peine à prendre mon parti, et que mon indétermination en fût plus excusable. Par là je reculais une rupture avec M. de Climal, et je gardais ce qu'il me donnait. (p. 39).[m]

This is the first time that the narrator has so clearly and lucidly attempted to disentangle Marianne's strategy. The two perspectives are kept distinct through the use of the present and the imperfect. She further demonstrates how far the young girl is prepared to go to deceive herself: "Je ne suis pas obligée de lire dans sa conscience, et je ne serai complice de rien, tant qu'il ne s'expliquera pas; ainsi j'attendrai qu'il me parle sans équivoque" (p. 40).[n] This is not the narrator's usual handling of the present through which she relives her past. Here the present is that of the heroine dialoguing with herself. The narrator also reveals what will become a characteristic attitude in Marianne, the refusal to act in order to shun all responsibility for what is going to happen: "je ne consultais que pour gagner du temps" and "j'attendrai." As the scene progresses the narrator insists on the importance of calculation in the heroine; what was only suggested at first is now unveiled: "Les hardes n'étaient pas encore en lieu de sûreté, et si je m'étais scandalisée trop tôt, j'aurais peut-être tout perdu" (p. 40).[o] Before the victim of M. de Climal's objectionable designs, Marianne now appears almost as the aggressor, as she consciously proceeds to deceive her seducer. Verbs suggesting deception—"je feignis," "je fis semblant," "en feignant de prendre le baiser" (pp. 41-42)—culminate in the heroine's triumph over her protector: "et je crois qu'il fut la dupe de ma petite finesse ..." (p. 42).[p] In spite of the narrator's desire to illuminate the heroine's motives, as she uncovers two different Mariannes—the virtuous and naive orphan as she appears to M. de Climal, and the already manipulative young coquette hiding behind a mask, and so good at seeing through others'—her irony is so mild, and tempered by so much affection for her younger self, that it becomes increasingly difficult to distinguish old Marianne's "I" from that of the protagonist.

The narrator's silence at Marianne's last rationalization of her acceptance of the clothes is rather disturbing: if she took the clothes, "c'était par un petit raisonnement que mes besoins et ma vanité m'avaient dicté, et qui n'avait rien pris sur la pureté de mes intentions. Mon raisonnement était sans doute une erreur, mais non pas un crime" (p. 45).[q] Given the careful monitoring of the heroine's thoughts granted by the narrator so far, it seems that the jesuitical distinction between *erreur* and *crime* would require further comments, which never come. The two "registers" mingle again. After Marianne breaks up with Climal, the episode of the acquisition of the clothes is paralleled by a scene in which Marianne's self-esteem requires that she return them. The heroine's rhetoric as she searches for a way to keep the dress echoes the argument she has used to accept it in the preceding episode; and predictably, the narrator's attitude also follows the previous pattern. As Marianne congratulates herself for finding the courage to return a dress which set off her beauty so well, the narrator ironically intervenes. But once more the irony is so mild that the emphasis is on the young girl's predicament, rather than on her casuistry: "Cependant le paquet s'avançait; et ce qui va vous réjouir, c'est qu'au milieu de ces idées si hautes, si courageuses, je ne laissais pas, chemin faisant, que de considérer ce linge en le pliant et de me dire en moi-même (mais si bas qu'à peine m'entendais-je): Il est pourtant bien choisi; ce qui signifiait: c'est dommage de le quitter" (p. 131).[r] At the same time as the narrator exposes what Deloffre calls "le décalage entre la pensée formulée et le sentiment profond" [the gap between inner feeling and the thought expressed] (p. 131n), she downplays the protagonist's self-deception, winning her reader over through the playfulness of her style ("ce qui va vous réjouir"). When Marianne finally feels entitled to keep the dress, the narrator concludes: "Je la gardai donc, et sans scrupule, j'y étais autorisée par la raison même: l'art imperceptible de mes petits raisonnements m'avait conduit jusque-là, et je repris courage jusqu'à nouvel ordre" (p. 133).[s] The narrator's insistence on "raison" and "raisonnement" is evidently ironic, as she manages to convey the exact contrary to what she is writing. She is actually communicating on two levels with her reader, not unlike young Marianne with herself: on the one hand, the narrator sets off what can be considered specious in the young girl's rationalizations, and on the other hand, she invites her addressee to suspend all judgment and to admire the heroine's cleverness.

The two registers which have been delineated in the narrator's discourse only mirror the duality that is the substance of young Marianne's nature. As most of the commentators of *La Vie de Marianne* have observed,[29] the heroine's main problem is finding her place in society. Her awareness of being *déplacée* is at least as acute as Pamela's, and the word recurs in her vocabulary: "Il valait mieux qu'une fille comme moi mourût d'indigence que de vivre aussi déplacée que je l'étais" (p. 45), "Mais en vérité j'étais déplacée, et je n'étais pas faite pour être là" (p. 32).[*] These comments are sparked by Marianne's dissatisfaction during her stay at Mme. Dutour's. What renders her plight even more extreme than Pamela's is that she does not know who she is; her only certainty is that she deserves more than she has got: "Car je devrais sans comparaison être mieux que je ne suis" (p. 35).[*] Marianne's desire to be recognized and admired springs from this discrepancy between her situation and her conviction of her worth and superiority; she is torn between that uncertainty about her origins that renders others' *estime* so necessary ("On n'est sûr de rien dans l'état où j'étais," p. 241) and an instinctive assurance of her worth ("J'avais des grâces et de petites façons qui n'étaient pas d'un enfant ordinaire," p. 15).[*]

This need for recognition is what renders love so vital in Marianne's world. Her comments on Valville's love are illuminating in this respect: "J'en étais tendrement aimée, de cet homme, et c'est une grande douceur. Avec cela on est du moins *tranquille sur ce qu'on vaut*" (p. 190; my emphasis).[*]

---

[29] Among them Henri Coulet notes: "Pendant toute la période de sa vie qui nous est racontée, le problème qui se pose à Marianne est de trouver sa place" (*Marivaux romancier*, p. 223).

94

Marianne clearly looks upon Valville's love as a means to substantiate her own existence; it explains not only why she is so shattered when she becomes aware of his infidelity—she loses both a lover and her self-esteem—but also why she recovers as soon as she manages to demonstrate her superiority to him and to herself:

> Cette dignité de sentiments que je venais de montrer à mon infidèle, cette honte et cette humiliation que je laissais dans son coeur, cet étonnement où il devait être de la noblesse de mon procédé, enfin cette supériorité que mon âme venait de prendre sur la sienne ... tout cela me remuait d'un sentiment doux et flatteur; je me trouvais trop respectable pour n'être pas regrettée. (p. 407).[x]

Given the emphasis that she lays on showing her superiority, it comes as no surprise that performance should be the key issue in Marianne's memoirs. Like Pamela, she poses as an object for others to contemplate and admire. Showing herself off (the verbs "montrer" and "se montrer" recur throughout the novel) is one of Marianne's main activities in life as well as in writing; this attitude is exemplified in the scene at church early in the novel. The eyes of the worshipers are so many mirrors for the heroine: "A peine étais-je placée, que je fixai les yeux de tous les hommes. Je m'emparai de toute leur attention; mais ce n'était encore là que la moitié de mes honneurs, et les femmes me firent le reste" (p. 60).[y] Marianne can only see herself—and thus she can only come to exist—if she sees herself being seen. Her parading and display serve a purpose; they let her watch others watching her, and create herself in the exchange of glances: "J'en eus pour garant certain coup d'oeil que je leur avais vu jeter sur moi quand je m'avançai, et je compris fort bien tout ce qu'il y avait dans ce coup d'oeil-là" (p. 61).[z] Marianne's strutting before the mirror of others is not ordinary vanity, narcissism, or exhibitionism. These attitudes love the self as if it were an object, but an object already posited and existing. In imagining herself before the event, as she is getting ready for church, Marianne succumbs to her own charm as to the appeal of a separate person: "ma vanité voyait venir d'avance tous les regards qu'on allait jeter sur moi" (p. 60).[aa] But what counts in this self-love is the distance involved, and the closing of it: the spatial gap between the self and the observer's ideal, or the temporal gap of anticipation. The specular image is not yet the self, but rather a glorious being the self would like to be and is trying to capture. For Marianne, a foundling, this glorious self is that noble origin and identity she is convinced she possesses. When others admire her they aid her quest for this identity: the "ought" or "must be" becomes "is."

Once this unity is attained, Marianne may in turn become a disinterested observer, as when she notices Valville: "J'oubliais de lui plaire, et ne songeais qu'à le regarder" (p. 63). A visual dialogue ensues: "Aussi le regardais-je toujours en n'osant, et je ne sais ce que mes yeux lui dirent; mais les siens me firent une réponse si tendre qu'il fallait que les miens l'eussent méritée" (p. 65).[bb] Yet even here there is a mental division. Marianne both looks and does not dare look. An uncharacteristic blindness—"je ne sais ce que les miens lui dirent"—seems to replace her usual hyperconsciousness, as if for once she does not see herself. Yet she watches herself retroactively, and her delight in her own sexuality is allowed to appear by a logical presupposition—"il fallait que les miens l'eussent méritée." Marianne's metamorphosis, from a mere object offered to others' eyes into a subject able to see, has often been stressed by Marivaux's commentators. What should be emphasized is the rarity and fleetingness of the disinterested gaze or simple visual communication; as this passage shows, even in such privileged moments Marianne never fully loses her awareness of being watched. While Valville's attention prompts the narrator to say, "Cela me fit rougir, et me remua le coeur à un point qu'à peine m'aperçus-je de ce que je devenais" (p. 65),[cc] the recovery is immediate.

Paradoxically, Marianne can better see and be seen when she hides behind a mask, even at the beginning of her relationship with Valville. She must conceal her real motives and feelings, since it would be immodest for her to let Valville know that she is as attracted to him as he is to her; yet this concern for modesty shows that she is already less interested in Valville's love than in his opinion of her. The paradox goes further: in order to see herself and merge with her idealized self, she must undergo a split: she masks her feelings to observe without being seen, so that part of herself is detached and watching, gaining insight into the other's mind, while part is displayed. As the doctor and Valville examine her foot, Marianne is both actress and audience: "Pour moi je ne disais mot, et ne donnais aucun signe des observations clandestines que je faisais sur lui, il n'aurait pas été modeste de paraître soupçonner l'attrait qui l'attirait, et d'ailleurs j'aurais tout gâté si je lui avais laissé apercevoir que je comprenais ses petites façons" (p. 68).[dd] Even the unrefined Mme. Dutour detects this watcher within Marianne: "Vous êtes d'un naturel soupçonneux, Marianne, vous avez toujours l'esprit au guet" (p. 99).[ee]

This duplicity constitutes the entire foundation of social intercourse for Marianne. The same mental division can be noticed in her relationship with Mme. de Miran, which demonstrates both astute observation and deliberate blindness: "Je rougis, en la voyant d'avoir été surprise dans mes lamentations; et malgré la petite confusion que j'en avais, je *remarquai* pourtant qu'elle était contente de la physionomie que je lui *montrai* et que mon affliction la touchait. Tout cela était dans ses regards; ce qui fit que les miens (s'ils lui disaient ce que je sentais) devaient lui *paraître* aussi reconnaissants que timides" (p. 147; my emphasis).[ff] The visual exchange between Mme. de

Miran and Marianne here is very similar to the one with Val-ville. Even in moments of confusion, Marianne is ever aware of the impact she has on others. Her ideal self must appear to others so that she can be at one with this ideal self. She wins over Mme. de Miran because of her good looks at first, then through her sincerity and honesty, as she confesses that she is "la petite aventurière" (p. 176) who causes Mme. de Miran so many worries. This confession only reinforces the image she wants to project, as Mme. de Miran admires her frankness: "Voilà une belle âme, un beau caractère" (p. 180). Subse-quently Marianne will pattern her conduct to fit the image Mme. de Miran expects. For instance, she refuses to see Val-ville "afin que si Mme. de Miran le savait, elle m'en estimât d'avantage; ainsi mon refus n'était qu'une ruse" (p. 201).*gg*

Our perception of Marianne is, of course, affected by the voice of the narrator, who stresses her duality, but young Mar-ianne is well aware of her "ruse." Later in the book, after a long debate with herself, she decides to confess to Mme. de Miran that Mme. de Fare has unmasked her, and that this could compromise her marriage with Valville: "Je ne serais pas pardonnable si j'avais des ruses envers vous, et si je vous dissimulais une chose qui a de quoi vous détourner du dessein où vous êtes de nous marier ensemble" (p. 283).*hh* Mme. de Miran's reaction comes as expected: "Tu es une fille étonnante et [Valville] a raison de t'aimer" (p. 284).*ii* Marianne's duplicity here is obvious, but the narrator underlines it as she makes her narratee say: "Vous ne couriez aucun risque à être franche; vous deviez même y avoir pris goût, puisque vous ne vous étiez jamais trouvée que mieux de l'avoir été avec Mme. de Miran, et qu'elle avait toujours récompensé votre franchise" (p. 290).*jj*

It would be an oversimplification, however, to assume that Marianne's whole relationship with Mme. de Miran is based on hypocrisy. At the same time as the heroine works at manip-ulating others, she works at creating an image of herself for

98

herself as well. The mask of sincerity that she wears for Mme. de Miran both is and is not herself, since it not only produces the desired effect on her foster mother (and might therefore be seen as extrinsic and adopted for the circumstances), but also serves to reveal an existential capability or dimension of her character that is as intrinsic as any facet of it. This dichotomy between acting and watching accounts for the mixture of consciousness and unconsciousness that appears in the preceding quotes. Her relationship with Mme. de Miran finally becomes more fulfilling for Marianne than that with Valville because Mme. de Miran turns out to be a better mirror than her son.[30]

As we have seen, Marianne is dependent upon others to achieve her ideal self; as the narrator points out, "nous avons tous besoin des autres; nous naissons dans cette dépendance, et nous ne changerons rien à cela" (p. 221).[kk] She can only see herself through their mediation, which is exactly what Mme. de Miran provides, as Marianne constantly sees the ideal image of herself in her "mother's" eyes. Marianne repeatedly tells Mme. de Miran that she matters more than her son: "Vous savez, ma mère, que j'aime M. de Valville, mais mon coeur est encore plus à vous qu'à lui; ma reconnaissance pour vous m'est plus chère que mon amour" (p. 281).[ll] This declaration of Marianne's love for her "mother," among numerous similar ones (see especially pp. 335, 343), illuminates the essence of the heroine's love for the older woman through her use of the word "reconnaissance." The word of course means "gratitude," and Marianne certainly owes much to Mme. de Miran; but its second meaning of "recognition" takes on significance here, as it underlines the interdependence and the narcissistic quality of the relationship between the two women. Marianne does not say "vous m'êtes chère et je vous dois de la reconnaissance," but rather "ma reconnaissance m'est chère." The double

[30] For a discussion of women's friendship in *La Vie de Marianne*, see Todd's *Women's Friendship in Literature*, pp. 328-32.

meaning of the word brings to mind the duality in Marianne. What we have here is a double "reconnaissance": Marianne gratefully recognizes Mme. de Miran's kindness, and also values those noble feelings she recognizes in herself. Mme. de Miran thereby becomes the medium through which Marianne can reconcile the dual images she has of herself (ideal and actual), hence be herself; because of Mme. de Miran, Marianne can know herself (*se reconnaître*). Marianne becomes the mask that she is wearing.

In the case of less noble sentiments, however, the self repudiates them and dissociates itself from them, especially when Marianne refers to her *amour propre* or her *vanité*: "Il n'y a rien de consolant dans de pareilles peines, parce que c'est la vanité qui nous les cause, et que de soi-même on est incapable d'une détermination" (p. 79). . . . "Je trouvai un expédient dont ma misérable vanité fut contente parce qu'il ne prenait rien sur elle, et qu'il n'affligeait que mon coeur" (p. 71; cf. also pp. 59-60, 71, 76-77, 92).*mm*

Just as Marianne establishes the self as an inner critical agency which, with others' mediation, evaluates her actions and thereby effects the coincidence between the two visions of herself, it can be shown that the narrator uses her relationship with her narratee to consecrate her identification with her specular image. Through her writing Marianne offers herself as an object to be admired by her reader. This view is, of course, in contradiction with Marianne's alleged motives for writing, as she tells her reader(s) that she writes her story out of mere friendship, to satisfy her friend's curiosity: "Quand je vous ai fait le récit de quelques incidents de ma vie, je ne m'attendais pas, ma chère amie, que vous me prieriez de vous la donner toute entière; et d'en faire un livre à imprimer. . . . Mais enfin, puisque vous voulez que j'écrive mon histoire, et que c'est une chose que vous demandez à mon amitié, soyez satisfaite: J'aime encore mieux vous ennuyer que de vous refuser" (pp. 8-9).[nn] In *Le Paysan parvenu*, Jacob remarks that "on se voit dans son amour-propre,"[31] but as has been shown, one can see oneself only if one is loved and admired by others. In spite of the narrator's multiple reflections, we do not know much about her situation at the time of writing. What filters through her discourse, however, is a certain nostalgia for her past beauty: "J'ai eu un petit minois qui ne m'a pas mal coûté de folies, quoiqu'il ne paraisse guère les avoir méritées à la mine qu'il fait aujourd'hui: aussi il me fait pitié quand je le regarde, et je ne le regarde que par hasard; je ne lui fais presque plus cet honneur-là exprès" (p. 51).[oo] Given the part played by the heroine's good looks in her ascension in society, it is easy to assume that she feels the loss of her beauty as a loss of identity. What remains, however, is her intelligence, even though she declares, "à cette heure que mes agréments sont passés, je vois qu'on me trouve un esprit assez ordinaire" (p. 9).[pp] If the narrator no longer dares look in her mirror or see herself in the mirror of others' eyes anymore, she can at least conjure up her past existence through the mirror of her narratee. When, after relating how Marianne decides to give up Valville, the narrator exclaims: "Oh! voyez avec quelle complaisance je devais regarder ma belle âme, et combien de petites vanités intérieures devaient m'amuser et me distraire du souci que j'aurais pu prendre!" (p. 190),[qq] she relives the scene through her recipient ("voyez"), who thereby gives it reality.

Marianne's apologetically convoluted addresses to her narratee reflect the heroine's primping in front of her mirror: "Où voulez-vous que je prenne un style?" (p. 9), "mais peut-être que j'écris mal" (p. 57).[rr] Each part of the novel (that is, each letter) starts with the same disingenuous timidity: "Dites-moi, ma chère amie, ne serait-ce pas un peu par compliment que vous paraissez si curieuse de voir la suite de mon histoire?" (p.

[31] Marivaux, *Le Paysan parvenu* (Paris: Garnier-Flammarion, 1965), p. 229. Future references will be to this edition.

57).[ss] The narrator addresses her recipient with the same coyness as the heroine did Valville; or rather she becomes as lost in the contemplation of her own reflection while she supposedly addresses her friend, as did the young Marianne who entered the church in which she met Valville's eyes. Marianne the narrator is not just communicating with her addressee; there is a double level of signification, with one level a mask for the other. The narratee is a ficton for Marianne, a necessary device that permits her to exult in her own character, to be her own audience. For Marianne, writing is essentially performance through the other.

Just as the relationship of the narrator with her recipient mirrors that of the protagonist with her audience, the heroine's activity within the text heralds that of the mature narrator: Marianne recounts her story several times to various audiences. The story may vary slightly according to the audience, but its impact is always the same; Marianne not only consistently wins over her listeners, she is also careful to note the effect of her tale as she tells it. After telling her story to Mme. de Miran, she remarks: "Je ne mis point d'autre art que ma douleur, et qui fit son effet sur la dame en question" (p. 153).[tt] When she gives another version to Valville and his mother, she notes that "ma bienfaitrice et son fils, à cet endroit de mon discours, me parurent émus jusqu'aux larmes" (p. 195).[uu] Marianne is as successful at the minister's: "J'aperçus plusieurs personnes de la compagnie qui détournaient la tête pour s'essuyer les yeux; le ministre baissait les siens, et voulait cacher qu'il était ému" (p. 335).[vv] All these versions of Marianne's story can be compared to that given by the narrator; however different they may be, what they have in common is quite significant. In each instance the content of the story is less important than its enunciation. It does not really matter whether Marianne gives her listeners a manipulated version of herself.

Each time she tells her story she creates herself, and her story achieves reality through the impact it has on the audience.[32]

The precedence of speech over facts is set off by comparison of Marianne's story to Tervire's. From a thematic point of view, the nun's story is clearly a negative analogue to that of Marianne. Although both heroines share the same physical and moral qualities, Marianne is successful whereas Tervire is the victim of her selflessness. Tervire's story is not as gratuitous as some critics assume, and Marivaux did not insert it simply because interpolated stories were in fashion in the novel of the time. The nun's story has an important thematic and structural function in Marianne's memoirs. The meaning of Tervire's story lies in facts, in its content; she talks about herself as if she were relating somebody else's story. As she tells it to dissuade Marianne from becoming a nun, her own existence is not involved in the telling, it does not concern her actual self. In Marianne's case, on the contrary, the speech event—that is, the way the story is told—is more important than the narrated event. (This may account for the fact that she never completes her memoirs.) In other words, the narration of the story is in itself an action through which the narrator comes to life (her present self counts more than the past she is supposedly trying to recapture); it is an event that modifies the narrator's life.

This subordination of the narrated event to the speech event also applies to the heroine. When Marianne finally relates her story to Varthon, she appears to be an expert and hyperconscious narrator: "Mon récit devint intéressant; je le fis, de la meilleure foi du monde, dans un goût aussi noble que tragique; je parlai en déplorable victime du sort, en héroïne de roman, qui ne disait pourtant rien que de vrai, mais qui ornait

---

[32] For a useful commentary on the function of Marianne's various *récits* in the novel, see Annick Jugan's *Les Variations du récit dans "La Vie de Marianne" de Marivaux* (Paris: Klincksieck, 1978).

la vérité de tout ce qui pouvait la rendre touchante. . . . En un mot je ne mentis en rien, je n'en étais pas capable; mais je peignis dans le grand" (p. 356).*ww* This passage, as it illuminates both Marianne's character and the narrator's discourse, is a paradigm of the whole novel. "Je parlai . . . en héroïne de roman"—this is the key to Marianne. The emphasis is not on the circumstances of the heroine, but on style: "je peignis dans le grand." She does not say "mon récit *était* intéressant," but "*devint*"; although she does not lie, "[elle] n'en [est] pas capable," her story becomes "real" through her performed utterance of it to Varthon. This passage also presupposes a certain detachment of the teller, as Marianne—as opposed to Tervire again, who gets lost in the content of her tale—projects herself out of her story to comment on it at the same time as she relates it. Marianne accumulates the functions of heroine, narrator, and author. Her words express an idea not unlike Diderot's theory of acting in "Le Paradoxe sur le comédien":

> Réfléchissez un instant sur ce qu'on appelle au théâtre être "vrai." Est-ce y montrer les choses comme elles sont en nature? Aucunement. Le vrai en ce sens ne serait que le commun. Qu'est-ce donc que le vrai de la scène? C'est la *conformité* des actions, des discours, de la figure, de la voix, du mouvement, du geste avec un *modèle idéal* imaginé par le poète, et souvent exagéré par le comédien (my emphasis).[33]

In the same way as, according to Diderot, the good actor imitates an "ideal model" on the stage, Marianne, who has been

---

[33] "Reflect a moment on what is called in the theater 'being realistic.' Does it occur when things are shown as they are in nature? Not at all. Realism in this sense would be no more than the merely common. Where, then, does the true realism of the stage lie? In the degree to which actions, speech, facial expressions, inflections, gestures, and movement all *conform* to an *ideal model* imagined by the playwright, and which the actor often exaggerates for effect." Diderot, "Le Paradoxe sur le comédien," in *Oeuvres esthétiques*, ed. Paul Vernière (Paris: Garnier, 1959), p. 317.

telling herself a romantic story from the beginning, patterns her behavior on this idealization.

It becomes irrelevant whether this story is a fiction or not when Marianne's behavior is construed as a result of her desire to live up to her own tale. By living it, by becoming it through her discourse, she makes it true. On two occasions Marianne herself is among the audience listening to her own story: once when it is told by Valville to Mlle. de Fare (pp. 266-67) and before that by Mme. de Miran at the minister's (pp. 228-29). The appropriation of her tale by others only reinforces its reality—and hers—as her story becomes another mirror in which she sees herself. This view of Marianne differs from Leo Spitzer's; Spitzer asserts that "Marianne devient dans le roman ce qu'elle est par son 'sang,' une aristocrate du *coeur* . . . elle devient ce qu'elle est . . . elle parvient à réaliser son moi . . . elle est une femme qui arrive, qui parvient à son vrai point de départ."[34] But it does not really explain the heroine's behavior (especially her relationship with others) to say that she "parvient à son vrai point de départ," since she does not know who she is when she is living her adventures; we never know whether hers is "un roman dans lequel s'explicite une force intérieure congénitale,"[35] as Spitzer would have it, since the narrator never elucidates the mystery of her origins. The closest she comes to it is when she says "il y a quinze ans que je ne savais pas encore si le sang d'où je sortais était noble ou non, si j'étais bâtarde ou légitime" (pp. 9-10).* The innateness that

[34] "Marianne becomes in the novel what she is by 'birthright,' an aristocrat of the heart . . . she becomes what she is . . . she manages to fulfill her identity . . . she is a woman who succeeds, who manages to reach her true point of departure." Leo Spitzer, "A propos de *La Vie de Marianne*," *Romanic Review* 44 (1953), p. 106. A somewhat similar point of view is expressed by Peter Brooks in his excellent chapter on *La Vie de Marianne* in *The Novel of Worldliness: Crébillon, Marivaux, Laclos, Stendhal*, (Princeton: Princeton University Press, 1969). See especially pp. 97-98.

[35] "A novel in which a congenital inner force gradually becomes unmistakable." Ibid., p. 108.

Leo Spitzer assumes for Marianne is in fact created by the heroine and the narrator through their various stories.

Leo Spitzer's interpretation of the character of Marianne is itself a denial of Georges Poulet's thesis that Marivaux's characters are "du rien qui se réfléchit à l'intérieur de rien, des reflets dans un miroir . . . un état de vacance et de paresse, cet état de néant préalable qui est celui de l'être qui, n'existant que par ses sensations, n'a pas encore de sensation."[36] Although Poulet's view could describe some characters of Marivaux's theater, it is too sweeping for Marianne. She is neither Spitzer's "présence pleine" nor Poulet's "void," but rather a character-novelist who weaves the web of her tale, integrating what happens to her into her basic fiction.

ALTHOUGH the ironic distance established between Jacob as narrator and Jacob as protagonist in *Le Paysan parvenu* is what is most often pointed out by the commentators of this novel (at least those concerned with its narrative voices),[37] the relationship between narrator and protagonist is at least as intricate in *Le Paysan parvenu* as in *La Vie de Marianne*. Jacob's irony toward his former self is indeed much more biting than Marianne's, and accounts for the comic tone of the novel. Jacob does not always look at the peasant he once was with the same smiling indulgence as Marianne the narrator does on the heroine of her memoirs. Young Jacob, in fact, is often treated with the same ridicule as the other characters. One of the narrator's favorite targets is false piety; he exposes the Habert sisters' pretense of abstemiousness and the intemperance concealed by

[36] "The reverberations of nothing within nothingness, mere reflections in a mirror . . . a state of uncommitted idleness, that initial emptiness of the being who exists only through his sensations, but has yet to experience any." Georges Poulet, *Etudes sur le temps humain, II: La Distance intérieure*, (Paris: Plon, 1952), p. 1.

[37] In particular Ruth P. Thomas, "The Role of the Narrator in the Comic Tone of *Le Paysan parvenu*," *Romance Notes* 12, no. 1 (1970), 134-41.

their self-mystification (p. 63). But he is no more lenient toward his own conduct, which may be hypocrisy or blindness according to the degree of self-consciousness we attribute to Jacob at this point: "Je le priai même plus qu'à l'ordinaire, car on aime tant Dieu, quand on a besoin de lui! Je me couchai fort content de ma dévotion, et persuadé qu'elle était très méritoire" (p. 118).[a] In openly disparaging terms the narrator underlines his past foolishness: "En vrai benêt je saluais cet homme à chaque mot qu'il m'adressait" (p. 207).[b] The novel is studded with such instances of direct irony, though they tend to become less frequent toward the end of Jacob's memoirs.

Like Marianne, Jacob the narrator often sheds light on motives repressed by the protagonist. "J'en étais honteux; mais je tâchais de n'y prendre pas garde, afin d'avoir moins de tort" (p. 212).[c] The narrator takes pains to emphasize what part calculation plays in the protagonist's behavior: "Or j'étais encore en prison, et cela me rendait scrupuleux" (p. 148).[d] Like Marianne again, he is often careful to separate his present perspective of experience from the protagonist's, thereby highlighting the latter's voluntary blindness: "Je ne fis pourtant pas alors cette réflexion; je la fais seulement à présent que j'écris; elle se présenta bien un peu, mais je refusais tout net d'y faire attention ..." (p. 237).[e] Although he is a less self-conscious stylist than Marianne, and consequently seldom comments on his own writing, like Marianne he often indulges in general reflections: "Mais dans ce monde toutes les vertus sont déplacées, aussi bien que les vices" (p. 51); "les dévots fâchent le monde, et les gens pieux l'édifient" (p. 58).[f]

The attitude of the narrator toward the protagonist is more often than not ambiguous. At times the protagonist appears ironically distanced from himself, while the narrator tends to subscribe to the protagonist's judgments. This is the case even early in the novel, in Jacob's relationship with Geneviève: "Peut-être fis-je mal en prenant l'argent de Geneviève. ... Cet

argent qu'elle m'offrait n'était pas chrétien, je ne l'ignorais pas.
. . . Mais je ne savais pas encore faire des réflexions si délicates,
mes principes de probité étaient encore fort courts; et il y a ap-
parence que Dieu me pardonna ce gain, car j'en fis un très bon
usage; il me profita beaucoup: j'en appris à écrire et l'arithmé-
tique, avec quoi, en partie, je suis parvenu dans la suite" (pp.
38-39).[g] The narrator characteristically expresses his reproba-
tion while simultaneously noting the extenuating circumstances of his past behavior. In the last sentence of the passage,
he further vindicates his action by echoing the typically eighteenth-century attitude that the ends justify the means. The
narrator follows the same pattern when he describes other relationships with the various characters who contributed to his
rise in society. But, as with Marianne, an attempt to evaluate
Jacob's character from a moralistic point of view does not lead
very far. Trying to find out whether the narrator and the protagonist are sincere or hypocritical leads to more ambiguity,
since Jacob (both Jacobs) condemns himself as sincerely as he
excuses his behavior. His motives for writing his memoirs are
not Rousseau's; his memoirs are no more a self-justification
than are Marianne's.

As in Marianne's case, several registers can be delineated in
the narrator's discourse; the point of observation oscillates all
the time. But the protagonist's relationship to himself is
equally ambiguous, and is further complicated by his relationship to the world. Unlike Marianne, however, who constantly
expresses her awareness of being "déplacée," Jacob seems not
to suffer from any problem of identity (though we will see that
such is really not the case). He knows and proclaims who he
is: a peasant. The narrator himself insists on the importance of
his origins from the start: "Le titre que je donne à mes Mémoires annonce ma naissance; je ne l'ai jamais dissimulée à qui
me l'a demandée, et il me semble qu'en tout temps Dieu ait
récompensé ma franchise là-dessus" (p. 26).[h] And indeed, to-

gether with his "bonne mine" (p. 29), his peasant origin seems to have been his main asset initially. Males as well as females like him for his rustic ingenuousness, which amuses the sophisticated high society as well as the servants: "Les domestiques m'affectionnèrent tout d'un coup; je disais hardiment mon sentiment sur tout ce qui s'offrait à mes yeux; et ce sentiment avait souvent un bon sens villageois qui faisait qu'on aimait à m'interroger" (p. 28).[i]

This refreshing spontaneity, however, soon becomes a weapon that Jacob turns to his advantage: "Je n'étais pas honteux des bêtises que je disais pourvu qu'elles fussent plaisantes; car à travers l'épaisseur de mon ignorance, je voyais qu'elles ne nuisaient jamais à un homme qui n'était pas obligé d'en savoir davantage" (p. 30).[j] Jacob acts and speaks according to his audience's preconceived idea of what can be expected from a peasant. In other words, Jacob plays a role from the start; he splits himself into director and actor. Much as for Marianne, for Jacob the self becomes a wondrous object to be admired: "Mon séjour à Paris m'avait un peu éclairci le teint et, ma foi! quand je fus équipé, Jacob avait fort bonne façon" p. 32).[k] The first part of this sentence is clearly the narrator's utterance, but the second part is more problematic. The switch from first to third person shows that the dissociation is not only between the narrator and the protagonist, that is, between the present and a fairly remote past, but exists also within the protagonist, who objectifies himself in order to contemplate his actions and their effect. This division is reminiscent of Marianne's "Je me proposais une conduite . . . digne de cette Marianne dont on faisait tant de cas" (*La Vie de Marianne*, p. 386).[l] This type of structure, in which "Jacob" occupies the position of complement, is more common in *Le Paysan parvenu* than in *La Vie de Marianne*. In the sentence, "Avant le dîner j'eus la joie de voir Jacob métamorphosé en cavalier" (p. 157),[m] one part of Jacob stands apart from the other to contemplate his progress.

This notion of progress, of gradation, throws light on what distinguishes Jacob from Marianne. In spite of their many similarities, they differ in that Marianne offers herself to others as an object to contemplate, so that she can be at one with her ideal self. Jacob, on the other hand, needs to separate himself from his former self in order to measure his progress. As the narrator points out, he needs his former self in order to enjoy the new one fully: "Car c'était en me regardant comme Jacob que j'étais si délicieusement étonné de me voir dans cet équipage; c'était de Jacob que M. de La Vallée empruntait toute sa joie. Ce moment-là n'était si doux qu'à cause du petit paysan" (p. 226).[n] The existential necessity of this split identity is underlined further when Jacob chooses a name to fit his new condition upon marrying Mlle. Habert. Retaining his peasant name of "Jacob" ("Il est beau ce nom-là . . . je m'y tiens," p. 85), he adds to it "de La Vallée." Though M. de La Vallée needs to recall his peasant personality in order to measure his progress, he also occasionally uses others for this purpose: "Je vécus là deux jours avec des voituriers qui me parurent très grossiers; et c'est que je ne l'étais plus tant, moi" (p. 53; cf. also p. 175).[o]

Hence the need to move on continually. He abandons Geneviève as soon as he feels superior to her, and it is evident that Mlle. Habert would have known the same fate had Marivaux finished his novel (her forthcoming death is already hinted at, p. 225), "parce que," as Jacob puts it, "ce ne serait pas ma pareille que j'aimerais, je ne m'en soucierais pas, ce serait quelque personne qui serait plus que moi; il n'y a que cela qui me ferait envie" (p. 133).[p] If Jacob is only able to love "quelque personne qui serait plus que [lui]," then the object of his desire is never attainable. This explains why his peasant self is so vital for him, since his anchor in the past serves as the only clear point of reference in the development of his life.

Similarly, the narrator's probing analysis of M. de La Vallée's feelings for Mme. de Ferval illuminates the protagonist's need for distance. He starts by remarking that he was more attracted to her rank than to her, because Mme. de Ferval "était une femme enfin qui nous tiraient, mon orgueil et moi, du néant où nous étions encore; car avant ce temps-là m'étais-je estimé quelque chose? avais-je senti ce que c'était qu'amour-propre?" (p. 135).[q] Jacob can separate himself from his self-esteem in order to see himself. Moreover, Mme. de Ferval's attentions literally give him birth. Characteristically, the protagonist cannot help comparing this relationship with the one he has with Mlle. Habert, "qui avait débuté par me dire que j'étais autant qu'elle, qui ne m'avait pas donné le temps de m'enorgueillir de sa conquête, et qu'à son bien près, je regardais comme mon égale. N'avais-je pas été son cousin? Le moyen après cela, de voir une distance sensible entre elle et moi?" (p. 135).[r] The narrator could not be more explicit. Others never lower themselves to him, rather they hoist him to their heights: "C'était de cette distance-là qu'on venait à moi, ou que je me trouvais tout d'un coup porté jusqu'à une personne qui n'aurait pas seulement dû savoir si j'étais au monde" (p. 135).[s]

Jacob's need for distance vis-à-vis himself and others is also expressed in his use of language. Whereas *Pamela* features a quest for literalness and exact correspondence between sign and meaning, Jacob uses language to abuse it. Taking it as a social mask, he modifies his language according to his audience. The signified for him has no intrinsic value, it is only a means of exchange with others, and is therefore utterly flexible. In Jacob's world the signified and the referent are totally independent. The narrator's remark about Mme. de Fécour illustrates this dichotomy: "Lui disiez-vous: j'ai du chagrin ou de la joie ... elle n'entrait dans votre situation qu'à cause du *mot* et non pas de la *chose*" (p. 169, my emphasis).[t] Jacob's recounting of his story to Mlle. Habert when he first meets her features an exact application of this dominance of sign over facts:

> Je conçus aussi que mon histoire était très bonne à lui raconter et très convenable.
>
> J'avais refusé d'épouser une belle fille que j'aimais, qui m'aimait et qui m'offrait ma fortune, et cela par un dégoût fier et pudique qui ne pouvait avoir frappé qu'une âme de bien et d'honneur. N'était-ce pas là un récit bien avantageux à lui faire? Et je le fis de mon mieux, d'une manière naïve, et comme on dit la vérité.
>
> Il me réussit, mon histoire lui plut tout à fait. (p. 56)."

This version of the affair with Geneviève obviously clashes with that given by the narrator a few pages before, and he himself acknowledges the discrepancy ("et comme on dit la vérité"). But this is irrelevent, since what counts is the manner in which the story is told. Because Mlle. Habert believes it, the story becomes true and Jacob becomes what he has said he is.

Jacob's relationships with others are entirely based on his conscious handling of language. He plays up his peasant side with Mlle. Habert, who shares his origins: "Je n'avais conservé cette tournure avec Mlle Habert que parce qu'elle me réussissait auprès d'elle, et que je lui avais dit *tout ce qui m'avait plu* à la faveur de ce langage rustique; mais il est certain que je parlais meilleur français quand je voulais" (p. 90)." He also capitalizes on his peasant side with noble ladies (for example, his first mistress and Mme. de Ferval) in order that his sexual aggressiveness may be expressed more openly without their taking offense or feeling threatened. (This ruse is also evident in the italicized part of Jacob's remark about Mlle. Habert above.) Here communication is double; the exchange between peasant and noble—a relation of inferior to superior—masks a sexual dialogue between hunter and prey, a reverse of superior and inferior. This double level of communicaton might be compared to those two levels, nonsense façade and aggressive intention, which Freud finds in jokes.[38] In relations with his first mistress, Jacob plays on the two levels instinctively, but with Mme. de Ferval he is quite aware of what he is doing; and so is she, according to the narrator: "et je vis que, toute réflexion faite, elle était bien aise de cette grossièreté qui m'était échappée; c'était une marque que je comprenais ses sentiments, et cela lui épargnait les détours quelle aurait été obligée de prendre une autre fois pour me les dire" (pp. 134-35).[w]

In his relationships with men, however, Jacob downplays his peasant side. On his way to Versailles he travels with three men, and Jacob is less voluble than usual: "Je m'observai beaucoup sur mon langage, et tâchai de ne rien dire qui sentît le fils du fermier de campagne" (p. 177).[x] Jacob is as careful during his confrontaton with the elder Habert sister at the president's: "Je m'observai un peu sur le langage, soit dit en passant" (p. 123),[y] and he adopts the language of a petit bourgeois in order to win over the president. It is by his linguistic versatility, by his brilliance in manipulating language—as his eloquence and skillful play on the words "domestique" and "serviteur" (p. 124) demonstrate in the trial scene—that Jacob outwits society's system of signs and makes his way in the world. His conception of language is much more complicated than Pamela's. It does not consist in finding simple equivalents for things, or showing the self off to its best possible advantage (although this he also does). Jacob knows that the self is always many things. Mastery of language implies the use of the best system for the circumstances, or even of two simultaneous systems.

Visual language is, of course, also represented in Jacob's multiplicity of languages; he always resorts to it along with words, but he never uses it so brilliantly as during the trial scene, where he wins over most of the audience before he even

[38] Sigmund Freud, *Jokes and Their Relation to the Unconscious*, trans. James Strachey (New York: Norton, 1963).

starts speaking: "J'avais dit des yeux à l'une: il y a plaisir à vous voir, et elle m'avait cru; à l'autre: Protégez-moi, et elle me l'avait promis. . . . Monsieur l'abbé même avait eu quelque part à mes attentions; . . . de sorte que j'avais déjà les deux tiers de mes juges pour moi, quand je commençai à parler" (p. 126).*

Because language carries no intrinsic truth for Jacob, one of its most fascinating characteristics is its dynamic, almost magical power. Instead of representing a preexisting concept, language creates it: discourse comes first, and truth follows after. For instance, when Jacob starts courting Mlle. Habert, he has no feelings for her, yet he literally talks himself into "loving" her: "J'avoue pourtant que je tâchai d'avoir l'air et le ton touchants, le ton d'un homme qui pleure, et que je voulus orner un peu la vérité; et ce qui est singulier, c'est que mon intention *me gagna tout le premier*. Je fis si bien que j'en fus *la dupe moi-même*, et je n'eus plus qu'à *me laisser aller* sans m'embarrasser de rien ajouter à ce que je sentais" (p. 96; my emphasis).*aa* Jacob's discourse has the same power in his courtship of Mme. de Fécour and Mme. de Ferval, convincing himself as well as the ladies in question of his love.

Objects in *Le Paysan parvenu* are endowed with a similar ability to transform their wielder. Jacob's outfits (not unlike Marianne's dress at the beginning) are not the sign of his condition, they only herald it. For instance, after changing his name, he explains to his wife that he needs a sword "pour être M. de La Vallée à forfait" (p. 155).*bb* The sword, however, soon becomes much more than Jacob had intended it to be. Like his words, it begins as an empty sign, but soon communicates to him a courage of which he was unaware, as he draws his brand-new weapon to rescue the comte d'Orsan: "Sans hésiter et sans aucune réflexion, me sentant une épée au côté, je la tire . . . et je vole comme un lion au secours du jeune homme" (pp. 227-28).*cc* Again, the narrator (who relives the scene, in the present tense) maintains the lack of premeditation on the protagonist's part. In such cases (for example, when Jacob talks himself into loving Mlle. Habert or rescues the count) the usual distinction between appearance and reality has no sense. (This is also why it would be fruitless to try to determine whether Jacob, M. de La Vallée, and the narrator are sincere or hypocritical.) This antithesis might be replaced by oxymoron, by talk of apparent reality or real appearances.

What is remarkable in this scene is that after his bout of heroism, M. de La Vallée no longer needs Jacob to delight in his accomplishments; it seems that his action has helped him unite his two selves. As Jacob affects a cool modesty, "un air de héros tranquille," the narrator observes: "je me regardais moi-même moins familièrement et avec plus de distinction qu'à l'ordinaire; et je n'étais plus ce petit polisson surpris de son bonheur, et qui trouvait tant de disproportion entre son aventure et lui. Ma foi! j'étais un *homme de mérite*, à qui la fortune *commençait à rendre justice*" (p. 229; my emphasis).*dd* These last words are reminiscent of Marianne's attitude toward herself at the beginning of her career. His discarding of his peasant self has already been heralded in a similar scene in which Jacob spontaneously steps aside to give the job he has been offered to Mme. d'Orville's ailing husband. After this first generous act, the narrator remarks: "ce discours quoique fort simple, n'était plus d'un paysan, comme vous voyez; on n'y sentait plus le jeune homme de village, mais seulement le jeune homme naïf et bon" (p. 193).*ee* These virtuous and heroic acts (prompted, as we have seen, by exterior forces) have the same function as Marianne's preconception of her high birth. Just as she has to live up to her tale (or reality) in order to effect the fusion with her ideal self, Jacob (or rather M. de La Vallée) will have to live up to this image of his worth projected to others. When the comte d'Orsan invites him to the theater, Jacob is acutely aware of this challenge: "Il faut prendre garde à vous, M. de La Vallée, et tâcher de parler bon français; vous êtes vêtu en enfant de famille, soutenez l'honneur du justaucorps, et que votre entretien réponde à votre figure, qui est passable" (p. 236).*ff* It is evident, however, that if Jacob feels the need to address himself in the third person, the fusion between his two selves is not completed. It is not sufficient to discard the peasant to become M. de La Vallée. In spite of this recent self-promotion to the status of "homme de mérite," Jacob is not really at one with his new identity, as his devastating experience at the theater demonstrates.

Jacob gets carried away as he drives to the Comédie in the comte d'Orsan's luxurious carriage: "Jusque-là je m'étais assez possédé, je ne m'étais pas tout à fait *perdu de vue*; mais ceci fut plus fort que moi, et la proposition d'être ainsi mené gaillardement à la Comédie me tourna entièrement la tête" (p. 237).*gg* Up to this moment Jacob has never "lost sight of himself," thanks to the distance he has carefully maintained between his various selves. He has relied on distance all along precisely in order to see himself. Ironically, when the distance between Jacob and M. de La Vallée, and between Jacob and the comte d'Orsan and his friends increases, Jacob loses control: "Nous étions arrivés à la Comédie. . . . Ici se dissipèrent toutes ces enflures de coeur dont je vous ai parlé, toutes ces fumées de vanité qui m'avaient monté à la tête" (p. 239).*hh* The supreme irony, of course, lies in the fact that it is at the theater, that temple of illusion, that Jacob gets lost in his various selves. There is no doing away with Jacob now; he comes back to the surface, not as the usual source of pleasure for M. de La Vallée, but as an embarrassment, as the peasant deprived of all his past charm and ingenuity: "Mes *yeux m'embarrassaient*, je ne savais *sur qui les arrêter*; je n'osais prendre la liberté de regarder les autres, de peur qu'on ne démêlât dans mon *peu d'assurance* que ce n'était pas à moi à avoir l'honneur d'être avec de si honnêtes gens, et que j'étais une *figure de contrebande* . . . et je tremblais

116

qu'on ne connût *à ma mine* que ce monsieur-là avait été *Jacob*"
(p. 240; my emphasis).[ii]

What had been Jacob's main weapon is turned against him
in this short scene. Whereas Jacob's gaze has heretofore mesmerized others, turning them into mirrors for his narcissistic
contemplation of his own image, now he does not know where
to look. His self-assurance is shattered; his "mine," which had
opened all the doors and hearts before, now becomes a threat
to him. Jacob suddenly becomes a fraud in his own eyes, a "figure de contrebande"; the narrator has never used such a de-
rogatory metaphor to describe the protagonist before. The
magnificent outfit lined with red silk, in which he had gloried
so much (p. 157), suddenly shrinks into "mon petit habit de
soie" (p. 240). Jacob's world of metamorphoses (the narrator
uses the word frequently) is completely shattered, deflated.

Jacob finally takes refuge in the darkness of the theater; on
the stage, in fact. "C'était une tragédie qu'on jouait, *Mithridate*,
s'il m'en souvient" (p. 241).[jj] Did Marivaux need to finish his
novel after this line? This scene constitutes the best conclusion
that he could have found. It is a debunking as well as a paradigm of the entire novel, since it is built on a dialectic between
inside and outside. Jacob has relied on what was exterior to
him all along: either his physical appearance, or a language
conditioned by what was expected of him by others. Here, on
the contrary, his impression of being inadequate comes from
inside ("le comte d'Orsan . . . continuait de parler sans s'apercevoir de ce qui se passait sur mon compte," p. 241),[kk] and it
shatters the façade. What is more serious is that this feeling of
inadequacy also shatters what had been posited as real from
the start: Jacob's peasant self (explicit from the first page of his
memoirs—"je n'ai jamais dissimulé [ma naissance]," p. 25).
The implication of this ending is that, in spite of his desire to
resuscitate his peasant self through the writing of his memoirs,
Jacob fails. He fails, because in the course of his progress, his

peasant attributes have been perverted, used as a mask; his identity has progressively become a façade.

In view of this last scene, Marie-Hélène Huet's assertion that "c'est du côté de Jacob qu'il faut chercher l'authenticité dans une aventure parallèle à l'ascension de La Vallée. . . . Jacob, fidèle à lui-même, coexiste avec l'intrigant La Vallée, et il faut croire que la brillante aventure de son double est aussi superficielle que la société qu'il fréquente, car jamais cette société n'oblige Jacob à oublier ses origines,"[39] is difficult to support. The outcome of Jacob's adventures, on the contrary, is that all preexisting authenticity is dissipated with the making of M. de La Vallée. Huet does not perceive that Jacob has been retained only as a tool, a yardstick, against which La Vallée could measure his progress. If M. de La Vallée needs Jacob to appreciate fully his new slippers and robe, he is ever careful to hide the real source of his pleasure from others: "Je songeai en moi-même qu'il ne fallait pas paraître aux autres ni si joyeux, ni si surpris . . . cette idée-là n'était bonne que chez moi, qui en faisais intérieurement la source de ma joie; mais il n'était pas nécessaire que les autres entrassent si avant dans le secret de mes plaisirs, ni sussent de quoi je les composais" (p. 226).[ll] Although Jacob does not forget his origins, he soon reaches the point where he tries more and more unsuccessfully to hide them. The peasant has to be concealed even from his wife, although it was his rustic naiveté which had first attracted her to him: "En pénétrant par elle-même toute ma joie, elle eût bien vu que c'était ce petit valet, ce petit paysan, ce petit misérable qui se trouvait si heureux d'avoir changé d'état, et il

---

[39] "Authenticity really resides in Jacob, whose adventure parallels the rise in society of La Vallée. . . . Jacob, his inner self unchanging, coexists with the scheming La Vallée, and his double's brilliant success is ultimately as superficial as the society in which he moves, for never does this society cause Jacob to forget his origins." In Marie-Hélène Huet, *Le Héros et son double* (Paris: José Corti, 1975), p. 42.

m'aurait été déplaisant qu'elle m'eût envisagé sous ces faces-là" (p. 226).*mm* When asked who he is, Jacob's reply is always conveniently vague; he is "le fils d'un honnête homme qui demeure à la campagne" (pp. 199, 239).*nn* His answer is not a lie, but it is sufficiently ambiguous.

Huet is the victim of the narrator's voluntarily ambiguous discourse, particularly when she claims that "contre La Vallée, au fond, Jacob a gagné. . . . Au terme de la conquête, le héros se retire à la campagne; son rôle joué, l'ombre de La Vallée s'estompe, et le paysan entreprend alors de le ressusciter dans l'acte d'écrire."[40] It would be more correct to reverse the terms and say rather that M. de La Vallée is trying to resuscitate or redeem the peasant through writing. This interpretation explains why the narrator insists so much on his origins at the outset, or why he dwells so lengthily on the example of his nephews who have denied their own father, without realizing that he is guilty of the same crime. Significantly, and not unlike Gil Blas, he will not be able to dredge up the memory of his true self. This is why his memoirs stop short with the scene at the Comédie, when it becomes clear that the rustic Jacob, having lost his sense of self in the course of his various metamorphoses, can no longer be restored.

IN order to show what unites *Pamela, La Vie de Marianne*, and *Le Paysan parvenu*, and what distinguishes them from the two works discussed in the preceding chapter, it is essential to clarify a critical terminology borrowed from philosophy. Despite its virtual ubiquitousness in discussions of eighteenth-century literature, this vocabulary is seldom applied with philosophical precision. Ontological questions of *être* and *paraître*, of truth or

---

[40] "Ultimately, Jacob manages to overcome La Vallée. . . . His conquest ended, the hero retires to the country; having played its role, the shadow of La Vallée disappears, leaving the peasant to attempt to resurrect La Vallée through the act of writing." Ibid., pp. 44, 48.

untruth as the appearance or concealment of being, ask: what is the being—the mode of reality—of the mask or appearance, as adopted or presented by the character of the novel. That Marivaux's work demands such an approach is obvious from the volume of critical literature devoted to the mask, yet nowhere is the mask as such defined and distinguished from a being it would conceal.[41] Such discussions assume terms a priori and remain on the thematic level.

For this ontological vocabulary to avoid superficiality, it must correspond with the semiotic discourse introduced in the preceding chapter, in reference to Gil Blas and Moll Flanders. One link between these systems is that matters of being and appearance involve the social values of both. In the books we are examining, reality has a social character. Persons and actions are perceived according to recognized codes of values, or described in a structured language. Therefore, judgments involve not an independent referent, not an absolute reality, but a reality meaningful for a given society. What I have tried to show in relation to Gil Blas and Moll Flanders, and what I shall attempt to summarize here in regard to Pamela, Marianne, and Jacob, is how the system of social meanings functions: how the characters, by their words and actions, communicate in social intercourse, and how the problem of being and appearance is inextricably entwined with that of the creation of meaning.

Let us first cast in these terms what has been said of Gil Blas and Moll Flanders. *Gil Blas* depicts a world of deceit, of pure appearance. This appearance has lost whatever tie it originally had with being and has now supplanted it. In semiotic terms, Gil Blas moves in a world of signs without referents. Social interaction is logomachic and in this war of signs, the combat-

---

[41] One notable exception is Lionel Gossman's essay, "Literature and Society in the Early Enlightenment: The Case of Marivaux," *MLN* 82, no. 3 (May 1967), 306-33.

ants dupe each other by understanding which signs the other recognizes, and by proffering as bait that signifier (word or act) to which the other will attach the desired sense. For themselves, this signifier will have a quite different value: it serves to implicate the other in their schemes, and thus acquires an ironic meaning as the designater of those schemes. Successful deception depends on a strategy I have stressed in both *Gil Blas* and *Pamela*: accurate replication of a system of signs, faithful copying of what others expect, or correct usage of the language that provides others' frame of reference. The appearance that is the sign has only a social truth or being as *adequatio*, a correspondence to what is accepted and expected. On the other hand, this *paraître* is afflicted with a *non-être* or nonbeing, for which this double mode of signification (for deceiver and victim) is in part responsible. The sign has no being, it is merely the point of intersection between an orthodoxy (in the etymological sense) and an aggressive intention. Furthermore, both signifieds dissolve into a system of endlessly receding references: aggressive intention and orthodoxy arise as attempts to secure values that are empty, copies of models that are themselves copies, and so on in an infinite regression. Signifieds become signifiers, and there is no being beyond an indicative appearance, which has no being in and of itself: the signifier is a transparency, through which we should see the signified; here being is a decoy, promising something but never delivering.

As I have described her, Moll Flanders also copies existing signs and wears masks, but these masks or appearances are more explicitly false than in *Gil Blas*. The mask is not merely an appearance but also concealment and secrecy; it is antibeing rather than simply nonbeing. Moll's being—what she really is—is defined in opposition to her disguise. The signified transcends the signifiers that would express it, an ineffable mystery. (What Moll was at each stage of her life becomes a mask rejected by the narrator.) *Etre* is *non-paraître*. In a sense this

121

mystery has no determinable being; and yet, paradoxically, Moll's being *is* this rejection, a tension or movement rather than an essence. For this reason I have labeled Moll's relationship to her text that of a critic; Gil Blas, on the other hand, writes in order to master the endless chain of regression, in order to wrest it, by copying his story, into a circle where he can somehow find himself.

Several major differences in treatment of being and signification separate *Pamela, La Vie de Marianne*, and *Le Paysan parvenu* from Moll's and Gil Blas's stories. First, the relationship between being and appearance is closer and more complicated. Rather than being taken as falsity or nonbeing, appearance is inherently linked to being. The appearance—the image of herself and her situation that Pamela creates in her writing, or that noble creature Marianne self-consciously displays to others and sees in their eyes, or those masks that the successful Jacob wears—this appearance is not untrue, but rather a particular mode of being: being as a potential, being desired, being in the process of becoming what it is and will be. To *be* in society, being must appear and be recognized for what it is; appearance is thus the social face of being. Being becomes a meaning signified; it creates itself by self-imitation.

What separates the three books studied in this chapter is the nature of being in the world. In their society, or world, being takes a different form or plays a radically different role. Being is conditioned upon other people. In the world of deceit and trickery we find in *Gil Blas* and *Moll Flanders*, others are quite literally "taken in" by deception: absorbed as they are fooled, they lose their exteriority and become pawns in the deceiver's scheme. In *Pamela, La Vie de Marianne*, and *Le Paysan parvenu*, others must maintain their distance and otherness for the protagonist to succeed; they are, after all, impartial observers, witnesses, unbiased readers. They possess the objectivity of the mirror. This distinction may be correlated to that made in linguistics between language (*langue*) and speech (*parole*). Gil Blas and Moll Flanders move within and use a common social language, a system of values and appearances. This language can be used to parrot or echo (Gil Blas) or else to lie (Moll). Nevertheless, it is simply there, available and never problematic. Statements made using it are accepted—appearances are taken at face value—by the world in general, and we do not see speech acts or true communication, in which the utterances are received by others who react and respond to them. What counts in the three books I have examined in this chapter is this reaction and exchange. Others are necessary: their speech, their confirmation, establishes the identity of the protagonist.

In fact, exteriority becomes indispensable the moment we begin to talk about things signified and perceived, and not about some mystical experience of reality that cannot be defined or recaptured in the same form. If we can repeat an experience or perception of being—recall it or convey it—it must be defined within a system of distinctions (this, and not that), encoded as something to which we refer (something signified). It must have a definite appearance. It must move out into the world, in order to be grasped by others (and first, by the self as other: by the self-conscious self). It must receive confirmation, be *homologué*, seen as such, as identical to itself, in others' recognition. This explains what I have called the reflexive structure of *Pamela, La Vie de Marianne*, and *Le Paysan parvenu*: the dialogue of the *regard*, the glance moving out to the other and reflected or returned. Pamela presents herself, or rather *re*-presents herself, in her writing; Marianne does so in the graciousness of her person. Jacob shows himself doubly, representing or playing the peasant of his past and also that nobler figure others will confirm.

Self-consciousness furnishes a third major distinction between the books treated in this chapter and those discussed in the first. It imposes another level of signification, termed metalinguistic in the case of Pamela. In *Gil Blas* and *Moll Flanders*, signs are used or abused; but if there is another level beyond this referential signification, it must be inferred. What I have described as an implicit deconstruction of signification emerges from *Gil Blas*; from Moll's rejection of past images of herself, from her treatment of them as masks, we come to sense the inadequacy of signification. These conclusions might be categorized as metalinguistic or semiotic, since they refer to the nature of the code used. But in the novel they are not drawn by the characters themselves. In *Pamela, La Vie de Marianne*, and *Le Paysan parvenu*, on the other hand, this level of signification plays an integral part in what happens in the novel. The characters do, on one level, use signs in reference and communication; but just as important as the use of signs is the consciousness of how well the sign is used, of how well the communication (speech, action, and appearance) is received, of how others react to it, of how the mechanism of the sign is working.

Considered in this light, Pamela compulsively transforms reality into signification: writing letters, she copies reality, repeats it as a text. She even goes so far as to copy other letters. In her letters, reality appears more vividly and convincingly than it did in the world. Being appears only when it is signified, and the text finally displaces the world, as Mr. B. notes in calling his skirmishes with Pamela part of her "plots." Pamela's being is actually double. It is, on the one hand, her initial status as determined by society and, on the other, that identity she strives to achieve as wife and author. Her story is the emerging or appearing of this second identity, both *être* and *paraître*. Because it involves true being, Pamela must attain it by proper use of signs, by literalness of language, by exact correspondence. But since it is also appearance, an image in her text, Pamela must make it appear (as one says of a book being published, *"le livre paraît"*); she must create it and make it public, achieve social recognition. Metalinguistically, it is the acknowledged success of the first effort that makes the second possible.

As with Pamela, the truth of Marianne's being emerges in part from a Cartesian certainty, a clear and distinct idea of her nobler self akin to what Corneille's characters call their *gloire*. This moral force evolves into the later philosophical understanding of being as will. Marianne's story is one of modal auxiliaries: the development of her being involves a passage from *will* to *do*, until finally she can be—perform as—that noble creature she visualizes. Her life begins with the mystery of a lost origin, with a certainty attached to vagueness (an ill-defined nobility). Her mysterious origin suggests allegorically a mystical being that cannot appear, cannot become conscious, because it is not yet signified. It is only when Marianne manages to repeat and project this image, to see her appearance in others' eyes, that her identity is assured. With others' mediation appearance becomes being. Signification is publically accepted, an act of speech adds to the common language: Marianne's story is told by others. The mysterious origin, like Moll's secrets, can never be fully found and recovered; it always maintains a certain distance from the self as it appears. But in Marianne's parading before others and awareness of their watching her, this distance between the self and the mystery is in effect replaced by the distance between the self and the other. What is beyond her—the origin—finds a substitute in the objectivity of the other and the impersonality of the common language. I have tried to suggest how this certification of Marianne's identity as it is chronicled in the novel affects Marianne's relationship to her text—her need to write—and in some measure justifies the unfinished form of the book. Once Marianne finds acceptance in society, and once her noble image passes into common language, the development of her being—its appearing, its attainment of its characteristic appearance—is essentially complete. Her life need no longer interest us, nor does it demand the supplementary certification that Marianne as historian brings to her development. Yet this ultimate appearance of being must be sustained by continued social acceptance and the admiration of others. When Marianne ages, and that appearance begins inevitably to decay, she is compelled to turn elsewhere: to seek confirmation from her reader, to repeat in the unfolding of her story the same evolution, the same appearance of being she once lived.

Like Marianne and Pamela, Jacob is effectively double, both peasant and something else. Whereas for Marianne the "something else" took the form of a mysterious origin situated in an inaccessible past, an origin that survives only as certainty and will until it is re-created, for Jacob it is not so much mysterious as undefined and variable. Like a joker in a card game, Jacob can assume many values. This side of Jacob's being exists as a competence, in modal terms: what he *can* be. Like Marianne and Pamela, Jacob's new status is confirmed by others' reactions to him. And again, in *Le Paysan parvenu* there are two levels (at least) of signification: one in which Jacob uses signs to pass as La Vallée, and another metalinguistic level, in which Jacob congratulates himself on his excellent use (or rather abuse) of signs, on the catachresis that is successful deception. Jacob the peasant is essential to this structure: without this being, constantly retained, there can be no deception, no abuse of signs. There would be only the manipulation or copying of signs, and the novel would turn into the textual play that is *Gil Blas*. The interaction between Jacob's two beings creates the novel, as the title indicates.[42] We witness both the *paysan*, the unshakeable basis of reality, and that development or appearance of being that is the movement of *parvenu*. I have quoted Marivaux's own formulation of this interplay, as Jacob (or

[42] See Huet's *Le Héros et son double* for a penetrating discussion of the novel's title, pp. 31-33.

rather La Vallée) tells us that it is the peasant who enables him really to savor his new-found status. Furthermore I have pointed to those moments of the interplay at which Jacob's two selves reverse roles in regard to being and appearance—as Jacob, again like a joker or jester, deliberately acts the peasant in order to take liberties otherwise impossible. Appearance, as I have made clear, is not inherently false; it is the reproducible face of being. The bond between being and appearance constitutes the mask; as in the joke, one kind of being appears that another may act without appearing. When appearance loses its being, the joke turns to panic: Jacob's reaction at the Comédie, as if he had awakened in the hall of mirrors that is *Gil Blas*. Only by further reflection, by giving his life the fixity of writing, can he somehow hope to retrieve his substance, beginning with the confession or profession of allegiance to reality that opens his tale.

CHAPTER THREE
Tristram Shandy
Imitation as Paradox
and Joke

C AN *The Life and Opinions of Tristram Shandy, Gentleman*
be considered a fictive autobiography? In spite of the
book's title, and notwithstanding Tristram's profession early
in the novel—"I have undertaken, you see, to write not only
my life, but my opinions also; hoping and expecting that your
knowledge of my character, and of what kind of a mortal I
am, by the one, would give you a better relish of the other"[1]—
it is not until the third volume that Tristram is born. If we except Volume VII, in which the grown-up Tristram takes a trip
to France, the narrator does not take the protagonist beyond
the age of five; and since the novel closes on the amours of Uncle Toby and Widow Wadman, we may say that it ends before
the hero's birth. Indeed, as has been observed, we learn more
about his uncle Toby's model fortifications or his father's domestic frustrations than about Tristram's life in the six-
hundred-and-some pages of the narrator's "autobiography."[2]
If we turn to Tristram's "opinions," we find that they occupy
less space than Walter's. This probably accounts for Adam A.

[1] Laurence Sterne, *The Life and Opinions of Tristram Shandy, Gentleman*,
ed. James A. Work (New York: Odyssey Press, 1940), pp. 10-11. All subsequent references will be to this edition.
[2] Cf. Wayne Booth, "Did Sterne Complete *Tristram Shandy?*" *Modern
Philology* 48 (1961), p. 180.

128

Mendilow's description of *Tristram Shandy* as "more biography than autobiography."[3]

Yet Tristram sets out to respect the "rules" of first-person narratives. For instance, he justifies his knowledge of the circumstances of his begetting: "To my uncle Mr. *Toby Shandy* do I stand indebted for the preceding anecdote, to whom my father . . . had oft, and heavily complain'd of the injury" (p. 6). The narrator also takes pains to account for his birth in the country rather than in London by looking for his mother's marriage settlement, which he reproduces in full (pp. 38-40). In the first volumes of Tristram's "memoirs," the incidents related to his birth, christening, and early childhood are thus substantiated as tales told in the family, and the narrator may legitimately have heard about them from any member of the household. But often, and especially after Volume iv, Tristram does not bother to give his sources, and on several occasions goes so far as to describe what went on in the various characters' minds long before he was born. Thus, when in Volume vi he justifies his transcription of a conversation between Walter and Toby by saying, "my father was so highly pleased with one of these apologetical orations of my uncle *Toby's* . . . that he wrote it down before he went to bed" (p. 459), the explanation seems a parody of the very device, of carefully accounting for his sources, which the narrator had used and dismissed before.

As the preceding examples indicate, from the standpoint of the relationships between the narrator and the protagonist or between the narrator and the other characters—relationships on which most autobiographical writings hinge—*Tristram Shandy* is a highly anomalous kind of autobiography. The protagonist hardly exists as such, and a study centering on him yields little; however, an examination of Tristram's relation-

---

[3] Adam A. Mendilow, *Time and the Novel* (London: Nevill, 1952), p. 185.

ship to his text and his readers proves much more fruitful, and not without links to the memorialist's relationship to his or her writing we find in the novels of Richardson or Marivaux.

Although early in the novel Tristram acquaints his readers with the date of his birth ("On the fifth day of *November*, 1718, . . . was I *Tristram Shandy*, Gentleman, brought forth into this scurvy and disastrous world of ours," pp. 9-10), and even with that of his begetting ("I was begot in the night, betwixt the first *Sunday* and the first *Monday* in the Month of *March*, in the year of our Lord one thousand seven hundred and eighteen," p. 8), events that could constitute a conceivable beginning for an autobiography, it soon appears that the date of writing is at least as important for the narrator as that of his birth. Numerous references to the situation and time of writing are strewn throughout the narrative: "I am now writing this book for the edification of the world—which is *March 9, 1759*—" (p. 44); "That observation is my own;—and was struck out by me this very rainy day, *March 26, 1759*, and betwixt the hours of nine and ten in the morning" (p. 64); "And here am I sitting, this 12th day of *August*, 1766, in a purple jerkin and yellow pair of slippers, without either wig or cap on . . ." (p. 600). This insistence on the situation of enunciation renders the image of the narrator, wearing his purple jerkin and yellow slippers, much more vivid than that of the protagonist at any point in the narrative, so that the situation of enunciation, rather than the "small hero's" birth, becomes the starting-point for the chronology of the novel.

Time is, of course, a paramount element in any retrospective narrative, but never before had the emphasis on time played such an important part as in *Tristram Shandy*. Most of the critical studies dedicated to Sterne's masterpiece naturally deal with this issue, often treating Sterne's handling of time as a mechanism of narrative technique which becomes an end in

itself rather than a means to an end.[4] Although there is no denying that Tristram's numerous comments on his handling of
time (cf. p. 103) are often ironic, and can be related to the parodic intent of the book, his obsessive concern with time is
much more profound than appears at first. If he feels "obliged
continually to be going backwards and forwards to keep all
tight together in the reader's fancy" (p. 462), it is not merely to
dazzle the reader with the fireworks of his technique. As
much of philosophy has recognized, time is inseparable from
the concept of self; and as shall become clear, Tristram's obsession with time should be linked to the ontological function
of the act of writing. The reflexive structure of *Pamela, La Vie
de Marianne*, and *Le Paysan parvenu* is more explicit in *Tristram Shandy*, since the main story told in Tristram's memoirs
is that of its coming into being, to the extent that the work becomes the chronicle of its own creation, and through it, that of
its author's. Like Pamela, Tristram *re*-presents himself
through his writing, and we shall see that his preoccupation
with Toby's or Walter's activities before he was born is not so
much a digression as a concern with origin. In the preceding
chapter I have described how the self becomes aware of itself
through the medium of the other. Here I shall examine how
Tristram uses his book to define himself in relation to the
other, be it the Shandy community or the writer's audience.

By simultaneously stressing the dates of his conception and
birth, and those of the composition of his work, the narrator
immediately initiates a parallel between his own generation
and that of his book. Tristram's work also parallels his life, as
he intends to dedicate as many years to writing his book as to
living its content. This parallel is nowhere more explicit than

[4] Such a view is exemplified by Bertil Romberg's *Studies in the Narrative
Technique of the First-Person Novel* (Stockholm: Almquist and Wiksell,
1962), p. 110.

131

in the following famous passage, often interpreted as Tristram's acknowledgment that his enterprise is doomed to failure:

> I am this month one year older than I was this time
> twelve-month; and having got, as you perceive, almost
> into the middle of my fourth volume—and no farther
> than my first day's life—'tis demonstrative that I have
> three hundred and sixty-four days more life to write just
> now, than when I first set out; so that instead of advanc-
> ing, as a common writer, in my work with what I have
> been doing at it—on the contrary, I am just thrown so
> many volumes back—was every day of my life to be so
> busy as this—And why not?—and the transactions and
> opinions of it to take up as much description—And for
> what reason should they be cut short? as at this rate I
> should live 364 times faster than I should write—it must
> follow, an' please your worships, that the more I write,
> the more I shall have to write—and consequently, the
> more your worships read, the more your worships will
> have to read. (pp. 285-86)

There is no denying that a pervasive theme in *Tristram Shandy* is that of impotence and failure: failure to communicate; failure to achieve a goal, in the case of Walter Shandy; or simply sexual failure, which concerns all the Shandys, including their bull. Yet the above passage is not simply a recognition of failure.

Tristram does admit that he is unable to keep pace with time—that the end of his book recedes because it takes him more time to write than to live. While this amusing paradox can be interpreted as suggesting the impossibility or hopelessness of reaching the infinitely receding goal, it can also be seen in a more positive light. It is both a strategy of infinite temporizing, postponing indefinitely the undesired cessation of both the life and the writing. By passing so quickly from infinite writing to its corollary, infinite reading, and by presenting both in the present and future tenses rather than in the conditional, Tristram treats this prospect of infinite writing as something achievable and, since infinite reading exists, it is in some virtual sense perhaps already achieved. In fact, though Tristram does not say so explicitly, a further corollary to the infinity of writing is the immortality of the writer. His life has fused with the life he is recounting (and thus to some extent depends on it and is its corollary), and this perspective may explain the good cheer with which he faces the endlessness of his project: "I perceive I shall lead a fine life of it out of this self-same life of mine; or, in other words, shall lead a couple of fine lives together" (p. 286).

The parallel between his own conception and that of his work develops further as the mishaps and frustrations (mainly Walter's) that accompany Tristram's conception, birth, and baptism are echoed by the whimsical pattern of the book, which aims not only at frustrating the reader, but at reproducing the writer's apparent lack of control over the process of writing. In the same way as Walter could not prevent his son's nose from being crushed by the Papist Slop's forceps during delivery, so the narrator expresses his inability to determine what he is writing: "Ask my pen,—it governs me,—I govern it not—" (p. 40), or "—for I begin with writing the first sentence—and trusting to Almighty God for the second" (p. 540). The narrator even calls his work "rhapsodical" (p. 35), or "a wilderness" (p. 408), a book with neither beginning, middle, nor end, since the reader has to get to page 192 for the preface to it.

Yet this alleged lack of control is repeatedly undercut by Tristram's commentary on his *plan*: "I have constructed the main work and the adventitious parts of it with such intersections, and have so complicated and involved the digressive and progressive movements, one wheel within another, that the whole machine, in general, has kept a-going;—" (p. 73). Tristram's book is thus built on the tension between, on the one hand, his awareness of his lack of control over the events of his life (hence the necessity to investigate his past; that is, the past of his family, his genetic determination) as well as over the material of his book; and on the other, his assertion of the writer's power to tell his story in his own way, to play with language and chronology, and to control the reader. This duality, both an affirmation of control and an acknowledgment of failure, is both concealed and revealed through the narrator's handling of time. In his writing he both projects himself into the past (through the experiences of Toby and Walter) and into the future.

Since individuals define themselves in relation to others, Tristram's desire to understand his past and how it shaped his present accounts for the emphasis laid on the Shandy community, which represents his social background. When Tristram addresses himself as "Sport of small accidents, *Tristram Shandy*! that thou art and ever will be!" (p. 166), he merely espouses his father's conception of him: "Unhappy *Tristram*! child of wrath! child of decrepitude! interruption! mistake! and discontent!" (p. 296). Tristram's insistence that his work would be severely maimed without its "digressions" ("Digressions incontestably are the sunshine;—they are the life, the soul of reading;—take them out of this book for instance,— you might as well take the book along with them," p. 73) is therefore quite accurate. Thus the story of the grandfather's nose and the chapter about noses that follows it are not truly digressions, since they illuminate Walter's behavior after Doctor Slop's catastrophic obstetrical intervention, and how the incident may have shaped Tristrams's self-image. Similarly, the many pages dedicated to Toby's and Walter's idiosyncrasies appear necessary wheels turning within the larger wheel of Tristram's autobiography. This is further suggested by the temporal correlation between Walter Shandy's *Tristrapaedia* and Tristram's own book. As young Tristram grows faster than his father can write, Walter's educational treatise becomes obsolete before it can be completed, with the consequence for Tristram "that I was all that time totally neglected and abandoned to my mother; and what was almost as bad, by the very delay, the first part of the work, upon which my father had spent the most of his pains was rendered entirely useless,—everyday a page or two became of no consequence.—" (p. 375).

In the same manner the emphasis laid on Toby's hobby-horse may be explained on the surface by the fact that Toby is indirectly responsible for Tristram's various misfortunes. Among other things, he suggested the clause in his brother's marriage contract stipulating that Tristram's mother should lie in at Shandy Hall, with the consequence for Tristram that "I was doom'd, by marriage articles, to have my nose squeez'd as flat to my face, as if the destinies had actually spun me without one" (p. 41). Furthermore, the sash-window accident could have been avoided had Uncle Toby not needed new battering cannons for his "campaigns," so that Trim "had taken the two leaden weights from the nursery window" (p. 378); an action which brought forth Tristram's accidental circumcision and may be held responsible for his obsession with impotence. Even the last two volumes of Tristram's memoirs, which are entirely dedicated to his uncle's amours with Widow Wadman, and which have been heralded all along as the "choicest morsel of [his] whole story" (p. 337), can be considered as related to Tristram's own story, since, as he points out: "For my uncle *Toby's* amours running all the way in my head, they had the same effect upon me as if they had been my own—" (p. 629).

In the first volume, Tristram already links the peculiarity of

135

his personality and that of Uncle Toby to their genetic heritage, since Toby "derived the singularity of his temper more from blood, than either wind or water, or any modifications or combinations of them whatever: And I have, therefore, oft times wondered, that my father, tho' I believe he had his reasons for it, upon his observing some tokens of excentricity in my course when I was a boy,—should never once endeavour to account for them in this way; for all the SHANDY FAMILY were of an original character throughout;—I mean the males,—the females had no character at all,—" (p. 65). Each time Tristram refers to his uncle's story he further associates it with his own: "I make no doubt but I shall be able to go on with my uncle *Toby's* story, and my own, in a tolerable straight line" (p. 473). However, not only is he unable to narrate his uncle's story in a straight line (the story of Uncle Toby's amours is interrupted by that of Trim's amours, a story itself interrupted by that of his brother Tom with the Jewish widow, which is itself interrupted by that of the King of Bohemia), but the vital episodes of Toby's amours are withheld (Toby's entrance into Widow Wadman's house is followed by blank chapters 18 and 19; chapter 20 begins with a series of asterisks). Tristram confesses that "though I have all along been hastening toward this part of it [the story], with so much earnest desire, as well knowing it to be the choicest morsel of what I had to offer to the world, yet now that I am got to it, any one is welcome to take my pen, and go on with the story for me that will—I see the difficulties of the descriptions I'm going to give—and feel my want of powers" (p. 627). By constantly interrupting the "straight line" of Toby's story with comments on his own difficulties in telling it, that is, by shifting the emphasis from the narrative content to the narrative event, the narrator focuses on himself as well as on Toby, and the long-delayed "choicest morsel" of Tristram's book tells us more about the narrator than Toby, by highlighting his very reluctance to tell it, than any straight narrative would have done.

By promising and alluding to Toby's story all along, and then refusing to tell it, Tristram is not simply teasing the reader, or inviting him or her to participate in the narrative process. The reluctance of his narrative method reaches far deeper, as it mirrors Toby's inability to cope with Widow Wadman's sexuality, which itself must be linked to Tristram's own reluctance to deal with sexual matters in life (compare his timid allusion to his bedroom failure with dear Jenny: "I stood with my garters in my hand, reflecting upon what had *not* pass'd," pp. 517-18) as well as in his work. Although Tristram claims that Toby's "life was put in jeopardy by words" (p. 87), his uncle's tendency to substitute words for action at crucial moments is epitomized in the conclusion that he peremptorily proffers to Trim's story with the *Beguine*. As Trim reaches the climax of his courtship with the lady, "—my passion rose to the highest pitch—I seiz'd her hand—," Toby intervenes, "—And then, thou clapped'st it to thy lips, *Trim*—and madest a speech" (p. 575). This short exchange between Trim and Toby finds its development in the parallel courting scenes between Trim and Bridget in the kitchen, and Toby and the widow upstairs. While Trim launches a direct attack on Bridget, Toby takes refuge in words: "When he had told Mrs. *Wadman* once that he loved her, he let it alone, and left the matter to work after its own way" (p. 633), thus illustrating a view that Tristram attributes to the French, according to which "*talking of love, is making it*" (p. 634).

This phrase could serve as the emblem of Tristram's work. It certainly explains why precious little ever happens in the world that Tristram depicts; it also casts a new light on Tristram's digressions. They appear as an indirect way of designating what is impossible to say. In the same manner as Toby who, by making a speech, avoids having to actually (and physically) make love to Widow Wadman, by writing and constantly commenting upon what he is writing, Tristram avoids having to begin and hence to end.[5] What he is shunning is the origin: sex. Sex is never named outright but always alluded to in the novel, inevitably reminding Tristram of that sexual act—the primal scene—which is his origin. Having to begin implies having to die; thus, what is in fact the real story is his desire, which cannot be written. In this sense the whole book may be seen as an immense digression, since it endlessly circles around what cannot be named.[6] Dennis Porter is right when he remarks that "much of the curious pleasure in reading *Tristram Shandy* derives from the tension Sterne generated between Tristram's repeatedly avowed purpose of getting his story told and the manifold comic devices invented to frustrate that purpose."[7] In the same manner, the blanks in the text, the asterisks, the marbled and missing pages are not only devices to distance the reader from the narrative. They assume the same function as the digressions, but in reverse. If the very excess of the digressions may be construed as a kind of decoy or distraction from a point never made, the blanks in the text or the asterisks constitute a retreat in the face of what is not expressible. Tristram the rhetorician even provides the proper name (Aposiopesis) for that device which consists in the suppression of what the speaker or writer is about to say; he does so in describing Toby's utterance, "—My sister, mayhap, does not choose to let a man come so near her ****" (p. 100).

[5] For a discussion of the use of digression in *Tristram Shandy* as a refusal to name, see Alain Bony's excellent essay, "Terminologie chez Sterne," *Poétique* 29 (1977), 28-49.

[6] In Bony's terms, "Quant à ces digressions à l'intérieur de la digression qu'est le livre, ce sont les lieux du texte les plus éloignés du lieu originaire, de la même façon qu'elles paraissent perdre de vue l'histoire de la naissance de Tristram" (ibid., p. 40).

[7] Dennis Porter, "Fictions of Art and Life: *Tristram Shandy* and *Henry Brulard*," *MLN* 9, no. 6 (December 1976), 1264.

But as everything in Tristram's world has two "handles," his purpose here is to tease and underscore as well as to avoid.

Again the correlation between Tristram's subject matter and his manner of narrating should be underlined. Walter's fascination with rhetoric and Toby's with his model fortifications function as diversions or digressions for each of them. For Walter, "whose way was to force every event in nature into an hypothesis" (p. 644), words and speeches are not simply substitutes for actions, they also protect him from the risk of direct human contact—that is, they are Walter's version of a fortification. This is literally expressed in the chapters dealing with his research on noses: "When my father got home, he solaced himself with *Bruscambille* after the manner, in which, 'tis ten to one, your worship solaced yourself with your first mistress" (p. 225). Walter's hobbyhorse is a substitute for sex. His views on love are revealing in that respect; it is a passion "which couples and equals wise men with fools, and makes us come out of caverns and hiding-places more like satyrs and four-footed beasts than men" (p. 645). This is why "'twas the whole business of his life to keep all fancies of that kind [i.e., sexual ones] out of [his wife's] head" (p. 600). Walter Shandy makes love only "out of *principle*" (p. 116), as Toby puts it, and only once a month, as Tristram gives us to understand. It is remarkable that this conjugal duty is never referred to by its proper name; Walter alludes to this monthly ritual as his "beds of justice" (p. 434). Naming, or rather misnaming, empties the act of its threatening connotation. Speech and rhetoric armor Walter against the hard facts of life. The word, be it written or spoken, displaces the world, and a long speech on death appropriately makes Walter forget about his son Bobby's death, which has just been announced to him: "My son is dead!—so much the better;—'tis a shame in such a tempest to have but one anchor ... he had absolutely forgot my brother Bobby" (pp. 355-56).

As Tristram's digressions are an elision of what cannot be expressed, surrounding it instead with circumlocutions, similarly Toby's campaigns on his bowling green constitute a diversion from the wound he received at Namur, while necessarily referring to it. Toby's obsession with imitation battles and sieges replaces sexual power. Like Walter's rhetoric, his hobbyhorse is quite literally a substitute for a mistress; and it takes a European peace to make him aware of Widow Wadman's unsubtle attentions. Just as Tristram takes refuge in the "Aposiopesis" to escape from the unnamable, Uncle Toby shuns danger by whistling "Lillabullero" (cf. pp. 69, 164). Toby's digression is itself the source of several deviations from the usual course of events. Among other instances the sash-window falls on Tristram because its weights have been diverted from their usual use; Walter Shandy's boots meet the same fate, ending up on Toby's battlefield. Not only objects are diverted from their original meaning, so are words. Walter is wasting his breath when he tries to explain to his brother that "—every thing in this earthly world . . . has two handles" (p. 102). Should Toby hear that Doctor Slop is in the kitchen making a bridge, it would not occur to him that the bridge in question can be made for another purpose—Tristram's nose—than for his fortifications (p. 206). The highly comical verbal interchanges between Toby and Walter spring, on the one hand, from Toby's inability to see that each word—and especially military vocabulary—has at least two handles, and on the other, from Walter's belief that "the highest stretch of improvement a single word is capable of, is a high metaphor" (p. 405).

Needless to say, Toby's quandaries with words, and Walter's passion for rhetoric, only reflect Tristram's own interest in language. Early in the novel Tristram claims that it is "the unsteady uses of words which have perplexed the clearest and most exalted understandings" (p. 86); confusion "comes, as all

140

the world knows, from having a half a dozen words for one thing" (p. 542), so that "'tis one of the silliest things ... to darken your hypothesis by placing a number of tall, opake words, one before another, in a right line, betwixt your own and your reader's conception,—" (p. 200). Tristram's insistence on the problem of the gap between sign and referent culminates in the hilarious scene between Toby and Mrs. Wadman. Toby answers the widow's question about the exact location of his wound with, "you shall see the very place" (p. 623), upon which he asks Trim to fetch his map while the widow blushes, turns pale, and blushes again at the prospect of touching Uncle Toby's groin. Tristram's conclusion to the episode—"it shews what little knowledge is got by mere words" (p. 624)—together with the host of blurred exchanges between the various members of the Shandy community, have led several critics to infer that the central theme of *Tristram Shandy* is the impossibility of communication through language.[8]

However, like anything else in life or in his work, Tristram approaches this question of communication from various angles. His description and ample illustration of the inadequacy of words and the inability of language to communicate are only one facet of the larger and more vital question of the search for truth and origin. There is merit in James E. Swearingen's argument that Tristram's "real interest is in language as part of the continuum of his conscious being, not merely as a medium to convey that life to others."[9] In this sense Tristram's preoccupation with language is linked to his existential concern with Toby's and Walter's peculiarities.

If, according to Tristram, the unsteady use of words has ob-

[8] Cf. William V. Holtz, *Image and Immortality* (Providence: Brown University Press, 1970), pp. 70-74.
[9] James E. Swearingen, *Reflexivity in Tristram Shandy* (New Haven: Yale University Press, 1977), p. 140.

scured their meaning, the basis for adequate communication
can be found in careful definition of the words that one uses:

> Now, before I venture to make use of the word *Nose* a
> second time,—to avoid all confusion in what will be said
> upon it, in this interesting part of my story, it may not be
> amiss to explain my own meaning, and define with all
> possible exactness and precision, what I would willingly
> be understood to mean by the term: being of opinion,
> that 'tis owing to the negligence and perverseness of writ-
> ers, in despising this precaution, and to nothing else,—
> That all the polemical writings in divinity, are not as
> clear and demonstrative as upon a *Will o' the Wisp*, or any
> other sound part of philosophy, and natural pursuit. (pp.
> 217-18)

However, at the same time as Tristram ironically insists upon
the importance of definitions, he implies that they are entirely
useless, since communication presupposes a dialogue between
two parties who do not necessarily think the same thoughts:

> I define a nose, as follows,—intreating only beforehand,
> and beseeching my readers, both male and female, of
> what age, complexion, and condition soever, for the love
> of God and their own souls, to guard against the temp-
> tations and suggestions of the devil, and suffer him by no
> art or wile to put any other ideas into their minds, than
> what I put into my definition.—For by the word *Nose*,
> throughout all this long chapter of noses, and in every
> other part of my work, where the word *Nose* occurs,—I
> declare, by that word I mean a Nose, and nothing more,
> or less. (p. 218)

Tristram does several things here: of course, as is generally
pointed out about this famous passage, he makes sure that
even the obtuse reader will think of something else whenever

the word "nose" appears in his text; characteristically, he gives us no definition, but only a tautology. More importantly, Tristram implies that the meaning of words, however carefully defined, depends on the listener's own grid of ideas; since everybody rides a different hobbyhorse at Shandy Hall, words can pose formidable barriers between people.[10] In other terms, even careful definitions are defeated in a world in which words do not represent things, but ideas, which in turn signify things: "It is in the nature of an hypothesis, when once a man has conceived it, that it assimilates every thing to itself as proper nourishment; and, from the first moment of your begetting it, it generally grows the stronger by every thing you see, hear, read, or understand. This is of great use" (p. 151). Tristram here gives us an apt definition of the hobbyhorse, underlining the gap between words and reality as it occurs in the solipsistic world of Shandy Hall. But at the same time, with the last sentence, he expresses his delight in the very fluidity of language, which can be of great use if the speaker takes into account the precedence of the verbal context over the word itself. Words as such, in spite of their imprecision—there are so many synonyms and homonyms—would not constitute impassable barriers between people if the users remained aware of their various meanings, and refrained from depriving words of their multiple contexts in order to fit them into their own limited mental world: that is, if they accepted words as a medium of play.

Tristram suggests a way to reconcile his two distinctive positions in regard to communication. He has stated first, that with careful unambiguous definition, adequate communica-

[10] Tristram's preoccupations with language, of course, echo Sterne's contemporaries', and in particular Rousseau's (cf. his *Essai sur l'origine des langues*, although his anxiety about the "opacity" of words pervades his whole work). As oppposed to Rousseau, however, Sterne delights in the infinite possibilities offered by the fluidity of language.

tion is possible (in the sense of the *adequatio* or exact correspondence between a single intended meaning and a single perceived meaning); second, that communication is impossible, since words engender a plurality of meanings and each person will choose those that fit his or her preoccupations, with no guarantee that a common frame of reference will be established. But his delight in the fluidity and play of language suggests a compromise: communication must be thought of not as a transmission of a meaning, but as a social interaction, a game in which meanings are created in collaboration. It involves not a single fixed value, but a loose allusion, a sort of nucleus around which numerous possibilities spin. If we accept this view of communication we must revise or qualify that opposition between speech and action which we have so far used to analyze the role of the digressions in *Tristram Shandy*, and in fact the nature of the entire book when seen as a digression. For this social interaction is obviously a form of action, and by it things are acomplished on the level of the enunciation, utterance, or writing that do not merely repeat, replace, or postpone the content of the utterance.

It is remarkable that whatever communication occurs between Walter's and Toby's monadic universes is achieved through gestures.[11] In the same manner, Trim's gestures are always more eloquent than his words, as exemplified by his speech on death. Tristram's comment on his performance is "that of all the senses, the eye . . . has the quickest commerce with the soul,—gives a smarter stroke, and leaves something more inexpressible upon the fancy, than words can either convey—or sometimes get rid of. . . . And if Trim had not trusted

[11] Holtz underlines the importance of the tableaux and static poses in *Tristram Shandy*, which leads him to conclude that gestures are more effective than words for communication in Sterne's novel (*Image and Immortality*, p. 74).

more to his hat than his head—he had made nothing at all of it" (pp. 361-62).

The notion of communication as playing with nebulous meanings perhaps explains the significance and success of gestures as depicted in the book. (Gestures are themselves a paradoxical compromise or mediation between the unequivocal and immediate, and the ambiguous.) On the one hand a gesture is precise: it is the undeniable presence of the body, the presentation of a referent rather than the representation of a meaning. Yet it is also ambivalent: the gesture can be interpreted to suit the beholder's predisposition; the basic phenomenon can acquire a variety of shades of meaning in diverse frames of reference.

When we find a breakdown of communication in *Tristram Shandy*, it is not because of the failure of language itself, because of inadequate definition of words or the inevitable fluidity of language within divergent mental universes. It occurs, rather, because those involved forget the social role of language as play and are unable to cope with the play within language. It is not because of the inadequacy of words that Walter Shandy lives in isolation, it is because of the deterministic folly that leads him to invest words with a single, precise, and yet mystical meaning—for example, his faith in the influence of names (p. 54). By divorcing words from their play of contexts, arresting them and treating them as ends rather than as means toward an end—the social exchange of communication—he has divorced himself from himself, his world, and his audience. For him, a door that does not close properly does not prompt action, but rather becomes the object of long dissertations: "There was not a subject in the world upon which my father was so eloquent, as upon that of door-hinges.—And yet at the same time, he was certainly one of the greatest bubbles to them, I think, that history can produce: his rhetoric and conduct were at perpetual handy-cuffs" (p. 203).

Tristram, on the other hand, seeks to reconcile his rhetoric and his conduct, that is, his speech and his being. This is why he insists upon the social character of language from the start, since his search for self (or true being) passes through the channel of a true relationship with his audience.

> Writing, when properly managed, (as you may be sure I think mine is) is but a different name for conversation: As no one, who knows what he is about in good company, would venture to talk all;—so no author, who understands the just boundaries of decorum and good breeding, would presume to think all: The truest respect which you can pay to the reader's understanding, is to halve this matter amicably, and leave him something to imagine, in his turn, as well as yourself. (pp. 108-109).

Despite Tristram's amicable intention, despite his insistence on the gentlemanly qualities of decorum and good breeding, he in fact imposes his view of communication upon the reader, sometimes by trickery or cajolery, occasionally by force. As critics have generally missed the ontological concern that underlies the irony of this forcible liberation, their partial vision results in lopsided interpretations. For some, the reader is a mere puppet in Tristram's hands. Patricia Meyer Spacks, for instance, assumes that Tristram manipulates the reader in order to compensate for his powerlessness in controlling the events of his life: "The audience seems . . . to offer tempting possibilities for Tristram to exert the mastery unachievable elsewhere. . . . He bullies the reader, trying to control him through alternate poses of aggression and intimacy."[12] It is true that Tristram playfully asserts his power ("But courage! gentle reader!—I scorn it—'tis enough to have thee in my power—" p. 486), at times accusing his female reader of inat-

[12] Patricia Meyer Spacks, *Imagining a Self* (Cambridge: Harvard University Press, 1976), p. 139.

tentiveness and urging her to go back and reread the previous chapter while the narration proceeds without her (p. 56), at times doubting his reader's intellectual capabilities (p. 80), or repeatedly promising material that he never provides.

Yet this combination of bluff and mischief has its reasons: his treatment of the audience may parallel that of the Shandy community. The games that Tristram plays with the reader echo the pattern of expectation and disappointment examined earlier, upon which the entire book is built. Misleading his readers, guiding them into error, he deliberately creates the state of confused communication in which Shandy Hall flounders. Tristram's demonstration features a kind of Socratic hypocrisy. He first foists this approximate, pluralistic communication upon the reader and then feigns that it is the reader's own design. Just as the characters' reactions in the novel are determined by their personal preconceptions or hobbyhorses, so Tristram's use and abuse of double-entendre (for example, the chapters on noses and whiskers, which clearly play on several meanings despite Tristram's disclaimer) induce the reader to discover the double meaning, with the implication that the reader who does so bears all responsibility for such a perversion of language, and that the innocent author is unaware of any ambivalence: "—Fair and softly, gentle reader!—where is thy fancy carrying thee?—If there is truth in man, by my great grandfather's nose, I mean the external organ of smelling . . ." (p. 221).

Such participation of the reader in the double meaning of words has led John Preston to contend that "it is by confronting the reader with images of obsessed readers, people who are unable to resist obscene meanings, that Sterne can liberate the reader's imagination from such meanings."[13] Tristram, however, is as little concerned with liberating the reader—his du-

[13] John Preston, *The Created Self: The Reader's Role in Eighteenth-Century Fiction* (London: Heinemann, 1970), pp. 158-59.

bious catharsis liberates more *for* obscenity than *from* it—as with bullying the reader. More important to his endeavor is forcing the realization that there is no fixed meaning—or, as he puts it, no Truth—as such to be conveyed: "—Endless is the Search of Truth!" (p. 90). If Tristram wishes to "educate" the reader—and he does claim that "all good people, both male and female . . . , may be taught to think as well as read" (p. 57)—it is to the fact that education is doubly impossible, since it assumes an impossible transmission of impossible knowledge. In particular, humanity should not expect or desire total knowledge:

> Thus,—thus my fellow labourers and associates in this great harvest of our learning, now ripening before our eyes; thus it is, by slow steps of casual increase, that our knowledge physical, metaphysical, physiological, polemical, nautical, mathematical, aenigmatical, technical, biographical, romantical, chemical, and obstetrical, with fifty other branches of it, (most of 'em ending, as these do, in *ical*) have, for these two last centuries and more, gradually been creeping upwards towards that Ακμὴ of their perfections, From which, if we may form a conjecture from the advances of these last seven years, we cannot possibly be far off.
>
> When that happens, it is to be hoped, it will put an end to all kind of writings whatsoever;—the want of all kind of writing will put an end to all kind of reading;—and that in time, *As war begets poverty, poverty peace*,—must, in course, put an end to all kind of knowledge,—and then—we shall have all to begin over again; or in other words, be exactly where we started. (p. 64)

This description of Tristram's idea of knowledge is worth quoting in full for various reasons. In it he exposes his cyclical conception of learning and history as well as writing. This cyclism must be taken ironically; through a *reductio ad absurdum* argument, Tristram suggests that total knowledge is unattainable, as is the origin; humanity approaches it asymptotically. Not only does the hyperbolic curve have no upper limit of total knowledge, but it has no origin or starting point, because one can never fully know a first cause, never fully seize the ultimate roots or determining factors from which sprang the present situation. (As illustrated by Tristram's investigation of his ancestors under Henry VIII, in the chapter on noses, the regression of genealogy, doomed to failure, is the mirror image of one's advancing quest for truth.)

This ironic model of history is an image of Tristram's book, since he conceives of writing as reaching back into the past and forward into total knowledge as expression of the self. The humorous tone of the passage, paradigmatic of his method all along, emerges primarily in a Rabelesian parody of "opake" language. This litany of words ending in "-ical" is itself a *mise en abyme* of his treatment of the search for truth: the pretension of total knowledge, implicit in the technical names and in the positivistic belief in classification they reflect, here results in an accumulation that comically annihilates itself.

But this brilliant sampling of the correspondence existing between the content and the form of his book should not completely distract us from Tristram's insistence in this passage on fellowship and association. This theme heralds his desire, as mentioned previously, to share his endeavor with his recipient, and sets off the relation of reciprocity constantly present in his book. Characteristically, this appeal to his "fellow labourers and associates in this great harvest of our learning" is also ironic, and winds up denying itself along with the pretension of total knowledge. As elsewhere in his book, Tristram does not draw the reader into his work to convey information about himself and his world, for the relationship established with his various recipients is one of a joint game using language as a medium; even this appeal to the reader's imagination is a parody of communication, in which, as we shall see, the reader is only a pretext, an image of Tristram himself.

Long before Michael Riffaterre or Jonathan Culler emphasized the fact that the activity of the reader is as fundamental as the author's in a literary text, appeals to the reader were fairly common in eighteenth-century fiction. Addresses to the "gentle reader" are countless in Fielding's and Swift's works, to mention only British writers. But what distinguishes Sterne's works from others in this respect is the variety of the readers he involves. To start with, Tristram's reader is not sexless; if he sometimes irreverently admonishes the ill-defined assembly of his "dear creatures" (p. 195), he often carefully distinguishes between "Madam reader" and "Sir," between the "critik" and the "worships" or "Reverences." These persons often acquire a certain endearing individuality. "Sir Critik" is always carping (cf. p. 85), while the lady reader is not only absent-minded, as in a passage already mentioned (p. 56), but also far more libidinous than the male reader, and she has to be constantly reminded not to let herself be carried away by her imagination: "—Now don't let Satan, my dear girl, in this chapter, take advantage of any one spot of rising-ground to get astride of your imagination, if you can any ways help it" (p. 226; the sexual overtones of "spot of rising-ground"—the mons—and "get astride" make this equestrian image akin to Sterne's admonition regarding the meaning of "nose").

The variety of the inscribed readers' responses may be correlated to their diverse personalities; this is, of course, in keeping with the theory of communication represented in Tristram's book. But it is noteworthy that the response of Tristram's extradiegetic audience (i.e., posterity) confirms his recognition of several kinds of readers. Illustrating such divergence, William Holtz, for instance, writes that "through the wordy mists of *Tristram Shandy*, Trim emerges as the locus of verbal competence, of truly effective communication";[14] while John Preston takes the opposite view, seeing in Trim "a story-teller whose stories are always frustrated, and in this way he is a prototype, in the book, of the author-figure."[15]

When Tristram needs to tell the reader about his Uncle To-by's innocence and cleanliness of mind, with the implication that the reader is not mentally equipped to understand such ingenuousness, he always addresses himself to Madam reader (cf. pp. 163, 455). Tristram's readers so resemble the characters in his book—the female reader is as sexually threatening as Widow Wadman, and the Critik shares a lot with Walter Shandy—that the boundaries between readers and characters often become quite blurred, and it is not unusual for the reader to participate in the events related in the book: "I beg the reader will assist me here, to wheel my uncle Toby's ordnance behind the scenes,—" (p. 455). Later, Tristram provides two blank pages (pp. 470-71) for the reader to sketch the portrait of Widow Wadman. The reader's comments on the story are also numerous and petulent: "—How, in the name of wonder! could you write your uncle *Toby*, who, it seems, was a military man, and whom you have represented as no fool,—be at the same time such a confused, pudding-headed, muddle-headed fellow, as—Go look" (pp. 84-85; cf. also p. 511).

But most often Tristram seeks his readers' aid to help him disentangle himself from various narrative difficulties, such as problems of order. (Should he tell about Toby's campaigns on the bowling green before or after Toby's amours with Widow Wadman? "—What would your worships have me do in this case?—Tell it, Mr. *Shandy*, by all means.—You are a fool, *Tristram*, if you do" (p. 207; cf. also p. 235). In spite of Tris-tram's denials ("One would think I took pleasure in running

---

[14] Holtz, *Image and Immortality*, p. 72.
[15] Preston, *Created Self*, p. 175.

into difficulties of this kind, merely to make fresh experiments of getting out of 'em—Inconsiderate soul that thou art!" p. 545), these questions of narrative organization recur so often that they form an inherent part of the story he wants to tell; and it is no exaggeration to say that much of *Tristram Shandy* is dedicated to the description of the author at work (cf. p. 336). This emphasis on narrative technique rather than on the substance of the narrative proper furnishes the means of inscribing the reader in the text and of fostering the confusion between reader and character: "—Pray reach me my fool's cap—I fear you sit upon it, Madam—'tis under the cushion— I'll put it on—Bless me! you have had it upon your head this half hour" (p. 511). In such instances (cf. also p. 188) it is difficult to distinguish between character, reader, and author.

To the multiplicity of communication grids corresponds the multiplicity of readers; and just as there is no fixed barrier between readers and characters, so we cannot fully separate the narrator from the characters, as becomes clear in Tristram's investigation of his relatives' past and in the formal relationship between Tristram's book and Walter's *Tristrapaedia*. (The similarity between Tristram's and Walter's preoccupations is striking; they both rattle on endlessly on the subject of duration [p. 188] or on that of chapters [p. 389].) The implication is that there is no fixed meaning, and therefore no fixed being; author, characters, and readers tend to merge and exchange roles in *Tristram Shandy*, and Tristram incarnates their multiplicity. It is in this sense that the reader emerges as a pretext, as another figure of the author-narrator. Multiplicity and confusion extend as well to the history layered within the individual, and to the concept of time itself as the dimension in which being appears. There is no fixed point in time to which episodes bear reference. As the following passage demonstrates, the past is not more privileged than the future; Tristram encompasses both in the present of the enunciating "I":

Now this is the most puzzled skein of all—for in this last chapter, as far at least as it has help'd me through *Auxerre*, I have been getting forwards in two different journies together, and with the same dash of the pen—for I have got entirely out of *Auxerre* in this journey which I am writing now, and I am got halfway out of *Auxerre* in that which I shall write hereafter—There is but a certain degree of perfection in every thing; and by pushing at something beyond that, I have brought myself into such a situation, as no traveller ever stood before me; for I am at this moment walking across the market-place of *Auxerre* with my father and my uncle Toby, in our way back to dinner—and I am this moment also entering *Lyons* with my post-chaise broke into a thousand pieces—and I am moreover this moment in a handsome pavillion built by *Pringello*, upon the banks of the *Garonne*, which Mons. *Sligniac* has lent me, and where I now sit rhapsodizing all these affairs. (pp. 515-16)

In this chapter Tristram self-consciously and deliberately telescopes three different moments of his life through the present of his writing "I." It is a belated illustration of his remark in answer to the "hypercritic's" objection that Tristram had not allowed Obadiah enough time to reach Doctor Slop's house before they appear on the scene: "If the hypercritic . . .—should take upon him to insult over me for such a breach in the unity, or rather probability, of time;—I would remind him, that the idea of duration and of its simple modes, is got merely from the train and succession of our ideas" (p. 103). Tristram's ideas, of course, bear little resemblance to a "train" or "succession," and his juxtaposition of various moments in the space of consciousness (is it really a "present"?) reduces to absurdity the usual way of rendering time. Time is not a succession of moments strung in a line; Tristram perceives it in a synchronic way.

This synchrony is why it does not seem correct to assume that Tristram lives most fully through the story of the past,"[16] or that in his book, "the facts have an unholy tendency to unwind and trip up the past instead of begetting the future,"[17] that is, that the past is a compulsion or obsession in the neurotic sense, with the events cut off from the causality of history in the same way that the form of a symptom is disconnected from the underlying psychic conflict. In fact, if a book may be a "history-book . . . of what passes in a man's own mind" (p. 85), what passes in a man's mind has a peculiar relationship to past history. On the one hand Tristram, far from dwelling in the past, deliberately seeks to break with it: he vows to throw away the key to his study, renounce his library, and avoid plagiarism and "shewing the *relicks of learning*": "Shall we for ever make new books, as apothecaries make new mixtures, by pouring only out of one vessel into another?" (p. 343). But worse than this perpetual decanting, the linearity of the past— the causality that determines us—takes on the confining characteristics of a rope or locked groove: "Are we for ever to be twisting, and untwisting the same rope? for ever in the same track—for ever at the same pace?" (p. 343). Yet even this grand tirade is both decanting and cant; it, too, comes from Tristram's library, directly inspired by Burton's *Anatomy of Melancholy*, and, beyond Burton, who also borrowed, from remoter sources.

The self-contradictory impulses of this passage pose problems for the linearity they depict. The irony of the contradiction subverts Burton, makes a joke of compulsive repetition and innovation together. "Shewing" and eschewing the "relicks of learning," the individual consciousness, *at the same time* as it synchronizes different moments, is also split among dif-

---

[16] Ibid., p. 135.
[17] E. M. Forster, *Aspects of the Novel* (New York: Harvest Books, 1927), p. 111.

ferent moments and divergent impulses. It dwells less on or in the past than in the jokes or contradictions the past begets, as it trips itself up. If events seem to escape the causality of history, it is because history is not linear, but rather the more chaotic and disparate accumulation of the library, devoid of causality. Beneath consciousness is the archive of memory, the library or unconscious that is synchronic or timeless, ignoring past, present, and future. One cannot simply derive the self from genealogy, make it branch off from a family tree or a literary filiation. It emerges instead as a multiplicity synchronized, articulated simultaneously as an ironic contradiction or joke, not the least of which is the joke of itself: the ironic contradiction between a mind that unites, articulates, and synchronizes, and the mind that ramifies and disperses, following outward the profusion of its digressions.

Tristram's self is his library, his book—his book is a "book of books" (p. 218)—that is, the space of digression and synchronization that is writing. Whereas for Pamela, Jacob, or Marianne, appearance is a necessary adjunct to being, for Tristram being is fragmented, emerging in a kaleidoscopic shifting of appearances. His being is this play of multiplicity and simultaneity, expressible ideally in writing; it is this very possibility of appearing, the kaleidoscope that enables us to arrest its movement in an appearance, an image or interpretation that changes with our perspective. Like a joke, the contradictions of the past are repeated first by Tristram, then by the reader, who draws upon the heterogeneous library that is Tristram's book, finds pathways through it, links its parts synchronically. For this reason Tristram's "failure" is also his success. And the reader, continuing the process that is Tristram's writing, perpetuates his being as well, granting him a kind of immortality—". . . as long as I live or write (which in my case means the same thing)" (p. 162)—that unites living, writing, and reading in the same movement of endless digression.

155

CONCLUSION

TRISTRAM'S reference to his work as a "book of books" is
not only a jest. Rather, Sterne's masterpiece includes all
the uses of the first person delineated in the novels we examined earlier, and thus represents the proper culmination of this
study of the role and implications of this form. That the first
person simultaneously designates or harbors several distinct
voices in all the texts analyzed obliges us to reverse Benveniste's dictum. We took as our starting point his assertion that
"disant 'je,' je ne puis ne pas parler de moi." However, the
novels that have furnished the field of our investigation lead
inescapably to a different conclusion. Keeping Benveniste's
phraseology, we might state it in French as "disant 'je,' je ne
puis ne pas parler de quelqu'un d'autre."[1]

This paradox—the fact that the self cannot ever truly des-
ignate itself—is the crux of Sterne's *Tristram Shandy*. Tristram
demonstrates that although most first-person narratives pre-
suppose a coincidence between the two "I" 's—for what is the
search for the self if not the quest for unity?—the relationship
between the enunciation and the enunciated expression
(*énoncé*) is always problematic. The gap that exists between the
two "I" 's is unbridgeable; to it corresponds the space that exists between life and death, between the origin and the conclusion, the beginning and the end. Whereas in the novels examined in the first two chapters the narrators explore and
exploit this gap in their quest for unity, Tristram manages to
propagate this void in an "I" that cannot end.

[1] Or, as Tzvetan Todorov puts it, " 'Je' ne réduit pas deux à un mais de
deux fait trois." *Qu'est-ce que le structuralisme?* (Paris: Seuil, 1968), p. 66.

What cannot be said or named in *Tristram Shandy* is what refers to sex, to copulation, and (indirectly, recalling the primal scene, as psychoanalysis calls it) to the origin. For this reason it takes the narrator more than half his book to get Tristram to the point where he can be born, and why the book ends before his birth. The utterance that is not only taboo but also, in a literal sense, impossible, by reason of the transcendence of the self and the self's finitude that its historical framework implies—that is, some version of "I was born" based on first-hand knowledge—necessarily calls forth its historical corollary—the personal account that includes "I died." To avoid this end, Tristram, casting aside the prospect of total (historical) knowledge, deliberately leaves his book open, thereby refusing to die. This refusal to begin in order not to have to end also explains why impotence and fear of sex are structurally necessary in *Tristram Shandy*. The sexual innuendos that pervade Tristram's memoirs suggest the arbitrariness of language, which lets words carry several meanings simultaneously, including sexual ones. But jolly double-entendres also function as masks: Tristram's obvious delight in sexuality hides the deeper fear of sex that permeates his book and afflicts all its characters. His oblique references to sexuality make a joke of censorship, the same kind of joke as his copying of the gestures of his ancestors and of what has been written before. The fear, which must also be seen as a mock fear, makes a joke of the sexual intention, of both the sexual impulse and the fear of losing the self that paralysis conveys. The terms are relative: they exist only in relation to each other.

In this sense we may say that the sign has no more being in *Tristram Shandy* than in *Gil Blas*, since Tristram copies the convention, the censorship, and the fear in order to make a joke of copying. This consciousness of playing a game—this energy of laughter—fills the space left vacant in *Gil Blas*, a space that has its locus in the narrator's discourse. So the world of deceit of *Gil Blas* finds its equivalent in *Tristram Shandy*, but the deceit is only a literary game, in which it is the reader who is taken in, usually with full consent. I have previously described Gil Blas's universe as logomachic, since the characters use their discourse to fool and overwhelm each other. In Sterne's novel, at the level of plot and action, the only thing taken in is death. By his literary games, Tristram deceives finitude, frustrates frustration and impotence. He strives for or copies infinity in the way Gil Blas copies his various masters; but unlike Gil Blas, he undercuts his activity by accompanying it with the implied statement that it is in fact only a copy, part of a larger, ultimately irreproducible whole (cf. the twisted rope), and of an imperfect whole, at that. Even when Tristram tells the reader the date of his birth he knows full well that this knowledge is second-hand, and he is merely repeating what he has been told.

To the system of receding reference described in regard to *Gil Blas* corresponds Tristram's endlessly receding horizon of knowledge. As I have suggested, what ultimately moves Tristram is an attempt to recapture the origin, a desire for total knowledge of the self that includes its beginnings and ancestral determinations or causes. His effort turns into a quest to express that total knowledge suffused throughout the world. Everything that Tristram does happens within this framework and refers to this absolute horizon; but he is aware of the dilemma arising from the fact that the more we move toward this horizon, the more it expands (cf. p. 64). Fundamentally, the aim of Tristram's literary endeavors is more general: to express the nature of humanity. Yet as the library image shows, in its very aim and inspiration this project is plagiarizing from preceding texts, and any message it can deliver refers to another book, behind which there is still another, ad infinitum.

Whereas this copying is purely a play of illusion in *Gil Blas*, and the protagonist, entrapped in it, loses any shred of identity he might have had initially, in *Tristram Shandy* the copy is not entirely vacuous. Its space is filled with the consciousness of the joke, with laughter, but also with a delight in the form and substance of whatever is made fun of. Laughter is not merely a structural or algebraic operation, a simple ironic negation of something. It is a pleasure taken in the physicality, in the formal or substantial peculiarities of that which serves as a pretext for the joke, as much as in the joke itself. The laughter does not pass straightaway to the negation, as would be the case in the idealism of a dialectical reversal; rather, Tristram lingers in the enjoyment of his materials. As he puts it, his book is "wrote against any thing,—'tis wrote, an' please your worships, against the spleen; in order, by a more frequent and a more convulsive elevation and depression of the diaphragm, and the successations of the intercostal and abdominal muscles in laughter, to drive the *gall* and other *bitter juices* from the gall bladder, liver and sweet-bread of his majesty's subjects, with all the inimicitious passions which belong to them, down into their duodenums" (pp. 301-302). Whereas Gil Blas writes to master the chain of regression, Tristram only pretends to do so, since he, actually, jokingly feeds it.

In the same manner as Moll Flanders's being was described in the first chapter as that which is hidden, we can say that in *Tristram Shandy* one kind of being is always hiding another kind of being; the digression always covers something else. The total being as such is never fully revealed. What Tristram presents us with is never seen as truth as such; it is not false, nor is it simply true. Tristram's being appears only as a joke and a fragment. In this sense, as in *Moll Flanders, être* is *non-paraître*.

In the texts examined in the second chapter, appearance was described as potential being emerging; for Pamela, Marianne, and Jacob, being must appear and be recognized. In *Tristram Shandy* being is also a potential; it is whatever one can make out of the book or the life. Rather than being conceived as something desired, as is the case for Pamela, Marianne, and Jacob, being for Tristram is a movement toward the joke, a movement of approach which paradoxically disperses itself in the system of connections or associations that constitute the underlying innuendos of the joke.

In Richardson's and Marivaux's novels others are necessary, since their speech, their confirmation, establish the identity of the protagonist. It is by virtue of the mediation of others that appearance becomes being. For Tristram, too, being must appear in order to be recognized, but in his case appearance is a joke acknowledged as such. What was described as self-imitation in the second chapter also finds its equivalent in *Tristram Shandy*, as Tristram ironically portrays man in the act of endlessly "twisting and untwisting the same rope"; but again, in his case the ironic distance underlines the gap between the self and this activity, as Tristram opens up possibilities by parodying impossibility.

In *Tristram Shandy*, when others are taken in, the joke is responsible. Yet, just as in Richardson's and Marivaux's novels, others are also judges, others form the critical audience of Tristram's joke, and their reaction ratifies it as one. As in the novels discussed previously the audience also functions as a mirror, continuing the work of the author by reading, making new jokes, finding new itineraries, or eliciting new meanings.

In *La Vie de Marianne*, as in *Tristram Shandy*, the origin is never fully recoverable. Whereas in Marianne's case the distance between the self and the origin is converted into or replaced by the distance between the other and the self, in *Tristram Shandy* the distance between the unconscious (the library, memory that surfaces only in part) and the self—that is, the tension between multiplicity and unity—is replaced by the distance between the self and the other implicated in the joke. Just as in the case of Marianne, the relationship between the self and the other is a mixture of separation and complicity. In *Tristram Shandy* the relationship is that vague blend of distance and collaboration which I have described above.

Ultimately, the "book of books"—the one which, in its contradictions and multiplicity, harbors the others we have examined—suggests a further complication of Benveniste's affirmation, according to its own scheme of multiple negation. What links the "I" of the enunciated expression to that of the enunciation is the ambiguity of the other: distant and within the speaker, separate and collaborating with him or her in the performance of the joke. Saying "I," I always speak of someone else, and for someone else. But as Rimbaud and Sterne make clear, the "I" who speaks or writes is already someone else: that which, speaking through the enunciating "I," speaks of and to itself. Or as a hybrid of Rimbaud and Benveniste might put it, "disant 'je,' l'autre ne peut ne pas parler de soi."

APPENDIX

Gil Blas

[a] That which is real in terms of drama is the action taking place before us. That which is real in terms of narration is by no means the event described, but simply the act of narrating.

[b] Thus the events are not linked together: they follow one another. ... Likewise, human beings meet, grow apart, without influencing or reacting to one another.

[c] He was, perhaps (for I do not suggest this as a certainty), the most ignorant canon of the Chapter; and, indeed, I have heard say that he did not obtain his canonry by his erudition, but that he owed it entirely to the gratitude of a few kind-hearted nuns whose discreet messenger he had been, and who had sufficient influence to get priest's orders conferred upon him without examination.

[d] Then, with the air of an honorable man, he replied that in speaking of his conscience I was taking him at his weak point. In fact, it was not at his strongest, since instead of pricing the animal at ten or twelve pistoles, as my uncle had done, he was not ashamed to offer three ducats for it, which I took with as much pleasure as if I had got the best of the deal.

[e] I was a fool, I see so now, to have reasoned in that way.

[f] I asked for a room, and to offset the bad impression which my smock might give the landlord, I told him that despite my appearance, I was quite able to pay for my lodging.

[g] "O Heaven!" I exclaimed, "was there ever a fate as horrible as mine?"

[h] "O Fate!" I exclaimed, when I found myself alone, and in this condition, "full of strange adventures and disappointments."

[i] Instead of laying the blame for this unfortunate incident on myself alone, and believing it wouldn't have happened if I hadn't been so indiscreet as to confide in Majuelo without real cause, I blamed it all on innocent Fortune, and cursed my unlucky star a hundred times.

[j] But I was too irritable to bear the reproaches which a wise man in my place would only have laughed at, and so I lost my temper.

[k] Besides, Euphrasia had promised me nothing definite, which is perhaps the reason why she did not corrupt my fidelity.

163

[l] "Santillana," he said, "I wouldn't have thought you capable of composing such a state paper. Do you know that you have just written a document worthy of the pen of a Secretary of State?"

[m] I entered so thoroughly into the ideas of the new minister that, when he had read my work all the way through, he seemed surprised.

[n] "Your last sermon does not seem to me to be quite as powerful as those that preceeded it."
"I have been sorely deceived by your limited intelligence.... Farewell, Master Gil Blas, I wish you every kind of prosperity, with a little more tact."

[o] "The duties of a servant are troublesome, I admit, for a stupid person, but for a lad of intelligence they are highly attractive: a superior genius who enters into someone's service doesn't perform his duties in a rough way, like an idiot. He enters a house to rule, rather than to serve. He *begins by studying his master*; he accommodates himself to his faults, gains his confidence, and then *leads him by the nose*. Such has been my method of operation with my hospital governor. I soon had the hypocrite figured out; I saw he wanted to pass for a saint; I pretended to be his dupe—that costs nothing. *I went further; I copied him; and acting in his presence the same role* he played before others, I tricked the trickster, and gradually became his *factotum*."

[p] Far from exhorting me not to deceive anyone, they ought to have advised me not to allow myself to be deceived.

[q] I resolved to choose a gentleman's outfit, persuaded that *in this guise* I couldn't help but obtain some lucrative position.

[r] What pleasure I took in seeing myself so well decked out! My eyes couldn't get their fill, so to speak, of my appearance. Never did a peacock behold his plumage with greater satisfaction.

[s] I observed with astonishment that these three servants imitated their masters, and gave themselves the same airs.... They weren't content with assuming the manners of their masters, they even affected their language; and the rascals reproduced them so well that, except for a certain air of breeding, it was the same thing.

[t] It was worthwhile to see how we drank each other's health every instant, calling each other by our master's names ... they called me Silva, and we gradually got drunk under these borrowed names, as the gentlemen to whom they rightly belonged did.

u "See what it is to be in the service of people of quality! It elevates the mind: bourgeois positions don't have this effect."

v He vainly attempted to assume the pleasant manners of the cox-combs; it was a very poor copy of those excellent originals, or rather it was an idiot trying to give himself an air of nonchalance.

w And I was waited upon with various marks of respect, which gave me even more pleasure than the good food.

x Bad examples corrupted my morals; and as everything was then to be bought, I fell in with the prevailing custom; and, as everything is now given away, I have regained my integrity.

y This one seemed to me to be very energetic, bolder than a court page, and with a hint of roguishness. He took my fancy. His an-swers to my questions showed some intelligence; in fact, he seemed to be born for intriguing.

z Scipio, who imitated me so well that it might be said the copy was very near to the original. . . . I couldn't look on him but as another self.

aa On the other hand, I saw certain gentlemen who, annoyed by the scant attention paid to them, cursed in their very souls the neces-sity which forced them to cringe before that face. Others, how-ever, I saw who were laughing in their sleeves at his smug, self-satisfied airs. It was of no use to me to make these observations since I was incapable of profiting from them. I behaved the same way in my own house, and I hardly cared whether my arrogant behavior was praised or blamed, so long as I was obeyed.

bb "If a marquis, for three-quarters of the day, is by virtue of his birth superior to the actor, the actor during the other quarter rises above the marquis, by appearing as an emperor or a king. It seems to me that this is a compensation in nobility and greatness which brings us on a level with those at the court."

cc It seems to me that you are playing a rather nice role on the world's stage. . . . Like a stage hero who goes on his knees before his prin-cess. . . . "Instead of being disgusted with my turban, think of me rather as an actor, playing the part of a Turk on stage."

dd I'd better think of the part I am to play. . . . I even recalled all the passages in our stock-plays which might be useful to me in an in-terview, and do me credit.

ee "I have caught his spirit so well that I have already written certain abstract pieces which he would be willing to acknowledge. After his example *I hawk my wares* in rich people's houses, where I am excellently received, and where I deal with people who are not difficult to please."

ff "I have become an author, and have set myself up as a wit; I write verse and prose; I am equal to anything."

gg "By this convenience, which costs me nothing—as I possess the art of agreeing with those who are useful to me—I have gained the esteem and friendship of my patron. He has employed me to write a tragedy, for which he gave me the idea, and which I have composed under his eyes; if it succeeds, I shall owe part of my glory to his good advice."

hh "What charm does the situation of a poet hold for you? It seems to me that such people are despised in polite society, and that their meals do not come easily."

ii "But let me see what it contains," I continued, drawing it from my pocket, "let me just see how they've purified my lower-class blood." I therefore perused my patent, which ran thus: That the king, in acknowledgment of the zeal which I had displayed on more than one occasion for his service, and for the good of the State, had thought proper to confer on me a patent of nobility.

jj I suddenly *changed* with the good fortune, and listened only to my ambition and my vanity. . . . *Before I came to court* I was naturally compassionate and charitable; but such human weaknesses are not appropriate there, and my heart grew harder than flint.

kk I expected, therefore, to make my departure; but my expectation was deceived. My physicians, having abandoned me, left a fair field to nature, and thereby saved my life.

ll Scipio, therefore, went once more to Madrid; and I, awaiting his return, devoted myself to reading. . . . Above all, I liked good moral tracts, because in them I continually came across passages that flattered my hatred of the court and my taste for solitude.

mm So that Scipio might have nothing to reproach me with, I consented to act in the same way for three weeks.

La Vie de Marianne

a You want me to write down my story. . . . Do not forget you promised me.

b How many follies I shall soon be telling you about . . . !

c I remained in that situation a long while, screaming incessantly, without being able to disengage myself.

^d Although I should not have been able to explain to you at the time everything I have just related to you, I nevertheless felt it all keenly.

^e When I think about it now, I believe that my soul-searching was simply a device to give myself more time.

^f What is amazing is that I was quite pleased with his apology, which I accepted with utter simplicity and trust, never perceiving that it was in fact a repetition of the offense.

^g It seems that when one is first touched by it, love begins with that feeling of trust and the very sweetness of loving interferes with one's concern for being desirable. ... It is a fact of life that we strive harder to earn others' recognition than their respect.

^h My observation is by no means out of place; I have simply made it somewhat lengthier than I had originally intended.

ⁱ "Hmm! You speak of my heart, my dear child, but what about yours? Would you give it to me, if I asked you for it?" "Alas, you do indeed deserve it," I answered naively.

^j I saw in his eye such an ardent gleam that I had a sort of illumination ... the way M. Climal was looking at me suddenly seemed suspicious to me.

^k I was still not clear as to what was going on inside his soul, and his friendship, if such it might be supposed to be, was carried to such an extent that it certainly warranted my sacrificing my pride. I thus felt entitled to accept his offer of a dress.

^l I believe I should have refused, had I really been convinced that his feelings for me were those of love.

^m I searched my soul as to what I should do; and when I think about it now, I believe that my soul-searching was simply a device to give myself more time: my mind was teaming with a host of considerations, and I sought to complicate matters as much as possible, so that the task of coming to a decision might be all the more difficult, and my hesitancy and irresolution might seem more excusable. The upshot was that I managed to postpone breaking off with M. de Climal, and could keep what he was giving me.

ⁿ I have no obligation to know his conscience, and unless he is more explicit, I am innocent of encouraging him, so that I shall just wait for him to say something unmistakable.

^o The garments were not yet put away in a safe place, and if I had been too quick to make a scene, I might well have lost everything.

[p] I pretended . . . I made a pretense . . . deliberately appearing to take the kiss. . . . And I believe that he was taken in by my little trick.

[q] It was because my needs and my vanity had convinced me that it was acceptable to do so, without fear of tainting the purity of my intentions. My conviction was probably an error, but by no means a crime.

[r] All this time the bundle was taking shape, and what will amuse you is that in the midst of such lofty and noble reflections I could not help admiring the clothes as I was folding them, and kept saying to myself (though so faintly I could scarcely hear myself) how very well chosen they are! Which of course meant: what a pity to have to part with them!

[s] So I kept it, with no pangs of conscience, since reason itself gave me its blessing: skillfully and imperceptibly, my little arguments had won me over, and my resolve returned, at least for the moment.

[t] Better that a girl such as I die in poverty than live as out of place as I was; but in truth I was out of place, and I was not fit to be there.

[u] For it was certain that I should be better off than I was.

[v] One can be sure of nothing in the position I was in. . . . I had the graces and charming ways that were not at all those of an ordinary child.

[w] The man in question loved me tenderly, and that was of great consolation. It reassures one of one's worth.

[x] The dignity of feeling I had just displayed to my betrayer, the shame and humiliation I left in his heart, the amazement he must have felt at the nobility of my gesture, and, not least, the superiority my soul had just shown over his . . . it all stirred me with warm and flattering feelings. I thought myself too deserving of respect not to be missed.

[y] No sooner was I seated than I observed the eyes of all the men fixed upon me, for I had totally captured their attention; but their hommage was but half the honor paid me and the women paid me the rest.

[z] I was convinced that these were their thoughts by a glance I saw them cast me as I was coming in, and it was easy for me to know what was in those looks.

[aa] My vanity could see in advance all the stares I was bound to attract.

[bb] I forgot about charming him, all I wanted was to look at him. . . . Thus I found myself looking at him, yet scarcely daring to do so; and I have no idea what message he read in my eyes; but his eyes

gave me an answer so tender that mine must have done something to deserve it.

^{cc} It all made me blush and my heart was fluttering so violently that , I was barely aware of where I was or what I was doing.

^{dd} For my part I said not a word, and gave no indication that I was surreptitiously studying him; for modesty would not have permitted me to show my awareness of his attraction to me, and I should have spoiled everything if I had given the least hint that I understood his little artifice.

^{ee} "You have a suspicious nature, Marianne, your mind is always on the lookout."

^{ff} Upon seeing her I blushed at having been caught in my grieving, and despite the minor embarrassment of it, and my surprise, I *noticed* that she was pleased with the physiognomy I had *displayed* to her, and that my sorrow seemed to move her. All this I could see in her eyes; and if she could read in mine what I was feeling, the look I gave her must have *seemed* to her as full of gratitude as it was meek.

^{gg} . . . So that if Mme. de Miran should learn of it, she might respect me all the more; my refusal, therefore, was just a ruse.

^{hh} "It would be inexcusable for me to have any ulterior motives in my behavior toward you, or to endeavor to conceal from you a fact which might deter you from your intention to see us married."

ⁱⁱ "You are an astonishing girl, and [Valville] is right to love you."

^{jj} "You were not running any risk by being frank; in fact, you must have acquired a taste for candor, since it always proved beneficial in your relations with Mme. de Miran, and she had always rewarded your frankness."

^{kk} We all need others; we are born dependent on them, and that is something we shall never change.

^{ll} As you know, my dear mother, I love M. de Valville, but your claim to my heart is even stronger than his; the gratitude I feel toward you is dearer to me than my love for him.

^{mm} There is no consolation in such afflictions because they stem from vanity, and left to our own devices we cannot make up our minds. . . . I found an expedient; it satisfied my wretched vanity, which emerged unscathed, with only my heart having to bear the pain.

ⁿⁿ When I decided to give you an account of several episodes in my life, my dearest friend, I scarcely imagined that you would beg me to tell you the whole history of my existence, and even to have it published as a book. . . . Nevertheless, since you want me to write

my story down, and prevail upon me to do so in the name of our friendship, you can rest assured that I much prefer to bore you than to deny your request.

oo I had a pert little face which cost me not a few follies, although it is scarcely conceivable that it could have warranted them when you see it in its present condition; in fact I feel sorry for it when I look at it, and I only look at it inadvertently; that is the sort of honor I almost never pay it on purpose any more.

pp Now that my charms have vanished, I am aware that people find my wit rather ordinary.

qq Consider, my dear friend, with what complacency I delighted in the nobility of my own soul, and the myriad of little vanities that inwardly amused me and distracted me from the anguish I might have felt.

rr Where do you expect me to find a style? . . . But perhaps I write badly.

ss Tell me, my dear friend, are you not more or less trying to flatter me when you claim to be so eager to see the continuation of my story?

tt I put into it no adornment but my sorrow, and that had its impact on the lady in question.

uu My benefactor and her son, at this point of my account, seemed to me to be moved and tear-stricken.

vv I spied several among those assembled who were forced to turn away in order to dry their tears; the minister had lowered his gaze, and was struggling to hide the depth of his emotion.

ww My tale became interesting; I told it, in all good faith, with the accents of tragedy and nobility; I spoke as a helpless victim of her cruel fate, like a heroine of a novel, not saying anything that was not true, but embellishing the truth with those touches that made it more moving. . . . In short, I did not lie in the least, nor would I have been capable of lying; but I painted with flair and grandeur.

xx Fifteen years ago I still had no idea if my family was of noble blood or not, if I was born a bastard or legitimate.

Le Paysan parvenu

a I prayed to him even more than usual, for we love God most when we have need of him! I went to bed delighted with my piety, and sure that it was praiseworthy indeed.

^b Like a true simpleton I bowed to the man at every word he addressed to me.

^c It made me ashamed; but I paid no heed, or at least tried not to, so as to diminish my guilt.

^d I was still in prison, and hence full of scruples. . . .

^e This observation did not come to me then, but occurred to me just now, as I am writing this; I did have a vague awareness along these lines, but I adamantly refused to pay any attention to it . . .

^f But in this world all the virtues are misplaced, as well as the vices. . . . The religious humbugs are an offense to humanity, but the truly religious are its strength and glory.

^g Perhaps I did wrong in accepting money from Geneviève. . . . To take it was scarcely a Christian deed, that much I was aware of. . . . But I was still unschooled in the niceties of conscience, and my principles of probity were as yet rather hazy; furthermore, it is likely that God was willing to overlook my ill-gotten gain, for I put it to a very good use, and it was of great benefit to me. Thanks to it I learned to write and mastered arithmetic, and these skills were in part responsible for my later success.

^h The title I am using for my Memoirs announces the social rank to which I was born; I have never kept it a secret from anyone who inquired, and it has consistently been my experience that this candor has been rewarded by God.

ⁱ The servants took an immediate liking to me; I never hesitated to speak my mind about whatever caught my eye, and my opinions often reflected a plain country horse sense that made people eager to ask me questions.

^j I saw nothing to be ashamed of on the silly things I said as long as they were amusing; for thick as my ignorance was, I could nevertheless glimpse through it the fact that my stupidities were in no way damning for a man who could not be expected to know any better.

^k My stay in Paris had improved my complexion, and I must say, when I was all decked out, Jacob cut a handsome figure!

^l I set myself the task of behaving in a manner . . . worthy of the Marianne others found so remarkable.

^m Before dinner-time I had the pleasure of seeing Jacob transformed into a cavalier.

ⁿ For it was in looking at myself as Jacob that I could savor the surprise of seeing myself in such finery; it was Jacob who was the

source of M. de La Vallée's joy. The thrill was only so keen because of the little peasant.

[o] I stayed there for two days, among carters who struck me as exceedingly uncouth, no doubt because I myself was already less so.

[p] Because I could never love someone of my own rank; anyone I might care about would have to be above my station, and I could never feel attracted to someone who was not.

[q] Mme. de Ferval was, in short, a woman who could pull us up—my vanity and me—and make us more than the nothings we still were: for until that moment had I any inkling of my dignity or worth? Did I even have so much as a notion of self-esteem?

[r] Mlle. Habert, who had started by telling me that I was every bit as good as she was, and who had left me no time to feel the flush of pride in having won her, and whom, aside for her wealth, I considered merely my equal. Had I not been her cousin? How, after that, was I supposed to see any appreciable distance between her condition and mine?

[s] It was from that same distance that she came to me, or rather that I suddenly found myself raised up to join someone who should never even have been aware of my existence.

[t] Were you to say to her, "I feel miserable," or "I feel so joyful . . ." she could only sympathize with you because of the *word* and not because of the *thing* itself.

[u] It dawned on me that my story was quite proper, and an excellent one to tell her.

I had refused to marry a beautiful girl, whom I loved, and who loved me, though she offered me my fortune, and I had turned up my nose at the chance out of scruples of pride and modesty that only an honorable and worthy soul could have harbored. Wasn't that a flattering tale to tell? Indeed, I told it to her as best I could, artlessly, and as one speaks the truth.

It had the desired effect: she was quite taken with my story.

[v] The only reason I had stuck with such country talk in Mlle. Habert's company was that I found it so useful where she was concerned, since speaking like a bumpkin allowed me to say *whatever I pleased* to her: but I could certainly speak better French when I wanted to.

[w] And I understood that, all things considered, she was quite pleased with my inadvertent coarseness; it was a signal that I was aware of her feelings, and so spared her the trouble of going to great

lengths on some later occasion to reveal them to me in a veiled and indirect manner.

^x I watched my language carefully, and tried to say nothing that would smack of the son of a country farmer.

^y I paid attention to my language, needless to say.

^z My eyes were telling one lady, "you are a pleasure to behold," and she believed me, with another they begged, "protect me," and she had sworn to. . . . Even the abbot himself had not been neglected. . . . The upshot was that before I even began to speak I had already won over two-thirds of my judges.

^{aa} I freely confess that I tried to look and sound touching, like a man in tears, and that I was not above stretching the truth a bit; but the singular thing is that *I was myself carried away* by the emotion I was trying to convey. So convincing was I that *I was as taken in as she*, and had only *to give vent to my feelings* without striving to exaggerate them in the least.

^{bb} to be M. de La Vallée in earnest.

^{cc} Feeling a sword at my side, I unhesitantly and unthinkingly draw it . . . and rush like a lion to the aid of the young man.

^{dd} I even began to consider myself less familiarly than usual, and as more distinguished; no longer was I the little scamp astonished at his own good fortune, and who found such a disproportion between what he was and the adventure that had befallen him. I' faith, I was a *man of worth*, to whom fortune *was beginning to do justice*.

^{ee} Despite my lack of sophistication, my remarks were no longer those of a peasant, as you can see; nothing in them bore the mark of the young villager, but rather that of a young man who was simple and good.

^{ff} You are going to have to watch yourself carefully, M. de La Vallée, and try to speak decent French: you are dressed like a man of breeding; try to uphold the honor of your doublet, and may your speech make as satisfactory an impression as your face.

^{gg} Until then I had remained resonably self-possessed; I had never *lost sight of myself*; but now, on hearing his proposition, I could not help it; the idea of being driven off to the Comédie in such high style completely turned my head.

^{hh} We had arrived at the Comédie. . . . There the arrogance of my boastful heart was shaken, and all the vapors of vanity which had gone to my head were swiftly dissipated.

173

ii I had no idea *which way to turn*, or *on whom to cast my eyes*; I dared not take the liberty of looking squarely at others, lest my *nervousness* betray the fact that I had no right to be there in the company of such honorable gentlemen, and that I was a mere *impostor* . . . I could not keep from trembling, afraid that one might tell *simply by looking at me* that this particular gentleman had been *Jacob*.

jj There was a tragedy being performed; *Mithridate*, I think, if memory serves.

kk Count d'Orsan . . . continued speaking, oblivious to the scene taking place around me.

ll I thought to myself that I should do well never to let on to others how surprised or overjoyed I actually was . . . that idea was best kept to myself, and though it was precisely what inwardly delighted me, there was no need for others to be in on the secret of my joy, or to know whence it came or why.

mm Were she to discover herself how jubilant I was, she would have realized that the one so exultant at having risen in society was that poor wretch the valet, and the little peasant; and I should have found it extremely disagreeable for her to consider me in that light.

nn The son of a decent man who lives in the country.

BIBLIOGRAPHY

Defoe, Daniel. *Moll Flanders*. Edited by Edward Kelly. New York: Norton, 1973.

Lesage, Alain-René. *Histoire de Gil Blas de Santillane*. Edited by Maurice Bardon. Paris: Garnier, 1962.

————. *The History of Gil Blas of Santillana*. Translated by Henri Van Lann. Revised and completed by Henri Roberts. Philadelphia: The Bibliophilist's Library, 1898.

Marivaux, Pierre Carlet. *Le Paysan parvenu*. Paris: Garnier-Flammarion, 1965.

————. *La Vie de Marianne, ou les aventures de Madame la comtesse de ****. Edited by Frédéric Deloffre. Paris: Garnier, 1963.

Richardson, Samuel. *Clarissa*. London: Everyman, 1978.

————. *Pamela or Virtue Rewarded*. New York: Norton, 1958.

Sterne, Laurence. *The Life and Opinions of Tristram Shandy, Gentleman*. Edited by James A. Work. New York: Odyssey Press, 1940.

Adams, D. J. "Society and Self in 'Le Paysan Parvenu.' " *Forum for Modern Language Studies* 14 (1978), 378-86.

Alter, Robert. *Partial Magic*. Berkeley and Los Angeles: University of California Press, 1975.

————. *Rogue's Progress*. Cambridge: Harvard University Press, 1964.

Altman, Janet. *Epistolarity: Approaches to a Form*. Columbus: Ohio State University Press, 1982.

Anderson, Howard. "Tristram Shandy and the Reader's Imagination." *PMLA* 86 (1971), 966-73.

Bakhtin, Mikhail. *Problems of Dostoevsky's Poetics*. Translated by R. W. Rotsel. Ann Arbor, Mich.: Ardis, 1973.

Barguillet, Françoise. *Le Roman au XVIIIe siècle*. Paris: P.U.F., 1981.

Barthes, Roland. "Introduction à l'analyse structurale des récits." *Communications* 8 (1972), 1-27.

————. "To Write: An Intransitive Verb?" In *The Structuralists: From Marx to Lévi-Strauss*, edited by Richard De George and Fernande De George, pp. 155-67. New York: Doubleday/Anchor Books, 1972.

Bartmann, Susanna. "Defoe's Daydreaming: Becoming Moll Flanders." *Visible Language* 14, no. 3 (1980), 283-305.

Beaujour, Michel. "Autobiographie et autoportrait." *Poétique* 32 (1977), 442-58.

Benveniste, Emile. *Problèmes de linguistique générale.* Vol. 1. Paris: Gallimard, 1966.

Bersani, Leo. *A Future for Astyanax: Character and Desire in Literature.* Boston: Little, Brown, 1976.

Bjornson, Richard. *The Picaresque Hero.* Madison: University of Wisconsin Press, 1977.

Blanchard, Jean-Marc. "Of Cannibalism and Autobiography." *MLN* 93, no. 4 (May 1978), 654-76.

Blanchot, Maurice. *Le Livre à venir.* Paris: Gallimard, 1959.

Blondel, Jacques. "L'Amour dans *Pamela*: de l'affrontement à la découverte de soi." In *Etudes sur le 18e siècle.* Clermont-Ferrand: Assn. des Pubs. de la Faculté des Lettres, 1978.

Bonhôte, Nicolas. *Marivaux ou les machines de l'opéra.* Lausanne: Edition de l'Age de l'homme, 1974.

Bony, Alain. "Terminologie chez Sterne." *Poétique* 29 (1977), 28-49.

Booth, Wayne. "Did Sterne Complete *Tristram Shandy?*" *Modern Philology* 48 (1961), 172-83.

———. "Distance et point de vue: essai de classification." *Poétique* 4 (1970), 511-24.

———. *The Rhetoric of Fiction.* Chicago: Chicago University Press, 1961.

Borck, Jim. "One Woman's Prospects: Defoe's 'Moll Flanders' and the Ironies in Restoration Self-Image." *Forum* 17, no. 1 (1979), 10-16.

Bourgeacq, Jacques. *Art et technique de Marivaux dans Le Paysan parvenu.* Monte Carlo: Editions Regain, 1975.

Brady, Patrick. *Structuralist Perspectives in Criticism of Fiction.* Berne: Peter Lang, 1978.

Braudy, Leo. "Daniel Defoe and the Anxieties of Autobiography." *Genre* 6 (1973), 76-97.

Brooke-Rose, Christine. "Self-Confrontation and the Writer." *New Literary History* 9 (1977), 129-36.

Brooks, Douglas. "*Moll Flanders*: An Interpretation." *EIC* 19 (1969), 46-59.

Brooks, Peter. "Freud's Master Plot: Questions of Narrative." *Yale French Studies* 55-56 (1977), 285-96.

————. *The Novel of Worldliness: Crébillon, Marivaux, Laclos, Stendhal*. Princeton: Princeton University Press, 1969.

Brown, Homer O. "The Displaced Self in the Novels of Defoe." *ELH* 38 (1971), 562-90.

Bruss, Elizabeth W. *Autobiographical Acts: The Changing Situation of Literary Genre*. Baltimore: The Johns Hopkins University Press, 1976.

Buffon, Georges-Louis. *Oeuvres philosophiques*. Edited by Jean Piveteau. Paris: P.U.F., 1954.

Butor, Michel. *Essais sur le roman*. Paris: Gallimard, 1964.

Carrell, Susan Lee. *Le Soliloque de la passion féminine ou le dialogue illusoire*. Tübingen: G. Narr, 1982.

Castle, Terry. *Clarissa's Cyphers: Meaning and Description in Richardson's Clarissa*. Ithaca: Cornell University Press, 1982.

Chambers, Ross. *Story and Situation: Narrative Seduction and the Power of Fiction*. Minneapolis: University of Minnesota Press, 1984.

Charles, Michel. *Rhétorique de la lecture*. Paris: Seuil, 1977.

Chisholm, R. *The First Person: An Essay on Reference and Intentionality*. Minneapolis: University of Minnesota Press, 1981.

Columbus, Robert. "Conscious Artistry in *Moll Flanders*." *SEL* 3 (1963), 415-32.

Condillac, Etienne de. *Oeuvres philosophiques*. Edited by Georges Le Roy. 3 vols. Paris: P.U.F., 1947.

Coulet, Henri. *Marivaux romancier*. Paris: Armand Colin, 1975.

————. *Le Roman jusqu'à la Révolution*. 2 vols. Paris: Armand Colin, 1968.

Cowler, R., ed. *Twentieth-Century Interpretations of "Pamela."* Englewood Cliffs, N.J.: Prentice-Hall, 1969.

Cox, Stephen D. *"The Stranger Within Thee": Concepts of the Self in Late Eighteenth-Century Literature*. Pittsburgh: University of Pittsburgh Press, 1980.

Dallenbach, Lucien. *Récit spéculaire. essai sur la mise en abyme*. Paris: Seuil, 1978.

Dédéyan, Charles. *Lesage et Gil Blas*. 2 vols. Paris: Société d'édition d'enseignement supérieur, 1975.

Deloffre, Frédéric. "De Marianne à Jacob: les deux sexes du roman chez Marivaux." *L'Information littéraire* 11 (1959), 185-92.

————. *Marivaux et le Marivaudage*. Paris: Armand Colin, 1967.

de Man, Paul. "Autobiography as De-facement." *MLN* 94, no. 5 (Dec. 1979), 919-30.

Démoris, René. *Le Roman à la première personne*. Paris: Armand Colin, 1975.

Derrida, Jacques. *La Dissémination*. Paris: Seuil, 1972.

———. *L'Ecriture et la différence*. Paris: Seuil, 1967.

———. *La Voix et le phénomène*. Paris: P.U.F., 1967.

Diderot, Denis. "Paradoxe sur le comédien." In *Oeuvres esthétiques*, edited by Paul Vernière, pp. 299-381. Paris: Garnier, 1959.

Donovan, Robert A. "The Problem of *Pamela*, or Virtue Unrewarded." *SEL* 3 (1963), 377-95.

———. *The Shaping Vision: Imagination in the English Novel from Defoe to Dickens*. Ithaca: Cornell University Press, 1966.

Doody, Margaret. *A Natural Passion: A Study of the Novels of Samuel Richardson*. Oxford: Clarendon, 1974.

Dowling, William. "*Tristam Shandy*'s Phantom Audience." *Novel* 13 (1979), 284-95.

Dubois, Jean. "Enoncé et énonciation: analyse du discours." *Langages* 13 (1969), 100-110.

Ducroq, Jean, Suzy Halimi, and Maurice Levy. *Roman et société en Angleterre au dix-huitième siècle*. Paris: P.U.F., 1978.

Ducrot, Oswald. *Les Mots du discours*. Paris: Minuit, 1980.

Eagleton, Terry. *Literary Theory, an Introduction*. Minneapolis: University of Minnesota Press, 1983.

———. *The Rape of Clarissa*. Oxford: Basil Blackwell, 1982.

Eakin, John. *Fictions in Autobiography: Studies in the Art of Self-Invention*. Princeton: Princeton University Press, 1985.

Elliott, Robert C., ed. *Twentieth-Century Interpretations of "Moll Flanders."* Englewood Cliffs, N.J.: Prentice-Hall, 1970.

Erickson, Robert. "Moll's Fate: *Mother Midnight* and *Moll Flanders*." *Studies in Philology* 92 (1978), 75-100.

Fauchery, Pierre. *La Destinée féminine dans le roman européen du XVIIIème siècle*. Paris: Armand Colin, 1972.

Faye, Jean-Pierre. *Le Récit hunique*. Paris: Seuil, 1967.

Fellows, Otis. "Naissance et mort du roman épistolaire français." *XVIIIème siècle* 4 (1972), 17-38.

Fielding, Henry. *Joseph Andrews*. New York: Signet Classics, 1960.

Fluchère, Henri. *Laurence Sterne*. Paris: Gallimard, 1961.

Flynn, Carol Houlihan. *Samuel Richardson: A Man of Letters*. Princeton: Princeton University Press, 1982.

Folkenflik, Robert. "A Room of Pamela's Own." *ELH* 39 (1972), 585-96.

Forster, E. M. *Aspects of the Novel*. New York: Harvest Books, 1927.

Foucault, Michel. *Les Mots et les choses*. Paris: Gallimard, 1966.

Freud, Sigmund. *Jokes and Their Relation to the Unconscious*. Translated by James Strachey. New York: Norton, 1963.

Frye, Northrop. *Anatomy of Criticism*. Princeton: Princeton University Press, 1957.

Gasche, Rodolphe, ed. "Autobiography and the Problem of the Subject." Special issue, *MLN* 93, no. 4 (May 1978), 573-749.

Gazagne, Paul. *Marivaux par lui-même*. Paris: Seuil, 1954.

Gelley, Alexander. "Character and Person: On the Presentation of Self in Some Eighteenth-Century Novels." *The Eighteenth Century: Theory and Interpretation* 21 (1980), 109-27.

Genette, Gérard. *Figures II*. Paris: Seuil, 1963.

―――. *Figures III*. Paris: Seuil, 1972.

Girard, Alain. *Le Journal intime*. Paris: P.U.F., 1963.

Girard, René. "Marivaudage and Hypocrisy." *American Legion of Honor Magazine* 34 (1963), 163-74.

―――. *Mensonge romantique et vérité romanesque*. Paris: Grasset, 1961.

Glowiński, Michal. "On the First-Person Novel." *New Literary History* 9 (1977), 103-14.

Golden, Morris. *Richardson's Characters*. Ann Arbor: University of Michigan Press, 1963.

Goldnoff, David. "The Confessional Increment: A New Look at the I Narrator." *Journal of Aesthetics and Art Criticism* 28 (1969), 13-21.

Gossman, Lionel. "The History of the Self." *Diderot Studies* 16 (1973), 339-46.

―――. "The Innocent Art of Confession and Reverie." *Daedalus* 107 (1978), 59-77.

―――. "Literature and Society in the Early Enlightenment: The Case of Marivaux." *MLN* 82, no. 3 (May 1967), 306-33.

Gottlieb, Sidney. "*Tristram Shandy* and the Compulsion to Repeat." *Mid-Hudson Language Studies* 4 (1980), 69-81.

Greimas, Algirdas Julien. *Du Sens*. Paris: Seuil, 1970.

―――. *Sémantique structurale*. Paris: Larousse, 1966.

Haac, Oscar A. *Marivaux*. New York: Twayne, 1974.

179

Hardwick, Elizabeth. *Seduction and Betrayal: Women and Literature*. New York: Random House, 1974.

Hazard, Paul. *La Crise de la conscience européenne (1680-1719)*. Paris: Boivin, 1935.

Heidegger, Martin. *Introduction to Metaphysics*. Translated by Ralph Manheim. New Haven: Yale University Press, 1958.

Holtz, William V. *Image and Immortality*. Providence: Brown University Press, 1970.

Huet, Marie-Hélène. *Le Héros et son double*. Paris: José Corti, 1975.

Hume, David. *A Treatise of Human Nature*. Vol. 1. Edited by T. H. Green and T. H. Grose. London, 1890.

Hunter, Paul. "Response as Reformation: *Tristram Shandy* and the Art of Interruption." *Novel* 4 (1970), 132-46.

Hutcheon, Linda. "Modes et formes du narcissisme littéraire." *Poétique* 29 (1977), 90-106.

Jakobson, Roman. *Essai de linguistique générale*. Paris: Minuit, 1963.

James, Anthony E. *Daniel Defoe's Many Voices*. Amsterdam: Rodopi, 1972.

Jay, Paul L. "Being in the Text: Autobiography and the Problem of the Subject." *MLN* 97, no. 5 (Dec. 1982), 1045-63.

Jeffrey, David. "The Epistolary Format of *Pamela* and *Humphrey Clinker*." In *A Provision of Human Nature: Essays on Fielding and Others in Honor of Mirian Austin Locke*, pp. 101-17. Amherst: University of Massachusetts Press, 1976.

Jost, François. "Le je à la recherche de son identité." *Poétique* 24 (1975), 479-87.

Jugan, Annick. *Les Variations du récit dans "La Vie de Marianne" de Marivaux*. Paris: Klincksieck, 1978.

Karl, Frederick R. "Moll's Many-Colored Coat: Veil and Disguise in the Fiction of Defoe." *Studies in the Novel* 5 (1973), 86-97.

Kay, Carol. "On the Verge of Politics: Border Tactics for Eighteenth-Century English Studies." *Boundary* 2 (Winter 1984), 197-215.

Kempf, Roger. *Diderot et le roman*. Paris: Seuil, 1964.

Kermode, Frank. *The Art of Telling*. Cambridge: Harvard University Press, 1983.

―――. *The Sense of an Ending*. New York: Oxford University Press, 1967.

Kock, Philip. "On Marivaux's Expression: 'se donner la comédie.'" *Romanic Review* 54 (Feb. 1965), 22-29.

Kockelmans, Joseph J., ed. *Phenomenology, the Philosophy of Edmund Husserl and Its Interpretation*. New York: Doubleday, 1967.

Kristeva, Julia. "Le texte clos." In *Semeiotike: recherches pour une sémanalyse*, pp.113-43. Paris: Seuil, 1969.

Lamb, Jonathan. "Sterne's System of Imitation." *Modern Language Review* 76, no. 4 (1980), 794-810.

Lanser, Susan. *The Narrative Act: Point of View in Prose Fiction*. Princeton: Princeton University Press, 1981.

Larson, Kerry. " 'Naming the Writer': Exposure, Authority and Desire in *Pamela*." *Criticism* 23, no. 2 (1980), 126-40.

Laufer, Roger. *Lesage ou le métier de romancier*. Paris: Gallimard, 1971.

————. *Style Rococo, style des "Lumières."* Paris: José Corti, 1963.

Laurence-Anderson, Judith. "Changing Affective Life in 18th-Century England and Samuel Richardson's *Pamela*." *Studies in Eighteenth-Century Culture* 10 (1980), 445-56.

Lawall, Sarah. *Critics of Consciousness*, Cambridge: Harvard University Press, 1968.

Leavis, Frank. *The Great Tradition*. London: Chatto and Windus, 1948.

Lejeune, Philippe. *L'Autobiographie en France*. Paris: Armand Colin, 1971.

————. *Moi aussi*. Paris: Seuil, 1986.

————. "Autobiography in the Third Person." *New Literary History* 9 (1977), 27-50.

————. *Le Pacte autobiographique*. Paris: Seuil, 1975.

Lennard, J. Davis. *Factual Fictions: The Origins of the English Novel*. New York: Columbia University Press, 1983.

Levin, Lubbe. "Masque et identité dans *Le Paysan parvenu*." *Studies on Voltaire and the Eighteenth Century* 79 (1971), 177-92.

Lotringer, Sylvère. "Le Roman impossible." *Poétique* 3 (1970), 297-321.

Lynch, Lawrence W. *Eighteenth-Century French Novelists and the Novel*. York, S.C.: French Literature Publication Co., 1979.

Lyons, John O. *The Invention of the Self: The Hinge of Consciousness in the Eighteenth Century*. Carbondale: Southern Illinois University Press, 1978.

McCoy, Kathleen. "The Femininity of Moll Flanders." *Studies in Eighteenth-Century Culture* 7 (1977), 413-22.

McIntosh, Carey. "Pamela's Clothes." *ELH* 35 (1968), 75-83.

McKee, Patricia. "Unmastered Exchange in Richardson and Freud." *Boundary 2*, 12, no. 2 (Winter 1984), 171-96.

Marin, Louis. "The Autobiographical Interruption: About Stendhal's *Life of Henry Brulard*." *MLN* 93, no. 4 (May 1978), 597-617.

————. "Remarques critiques sur l'énonciation: la question du présent dans le discours." *MLN* 91, no. 5 (Oct. 1976), 939-51.

Mat, Michèle. "Espace, décor et temps dans les romans de Marivaux." *Studi Francesi* 58 (April 1976), 21-35.

Matthews, W., and R. Rader. *Autobiography, Biography, and the Novel*. Berkeley and Los Angeles: University of California Press, 1973.

Mauzi, Robert. *L'Idée du bonheur au XVIIIème siècle*. Paris: Armand Colin, 1967.

May, Georges. *Le Dilemme du roman au XVIIIème siècle*. New Haven: Yale University Press, 1963.

May, Gita. "Les Confessions, *roman picaresque?*" In *Zeitalter der Aufklärung: Gedächtnisschrift für Fritz Schalk*, edited by W. Hempel, pp. 236-53. Frankfurt am Main: Vittorio Klostermann, 1983.

Mehlman, Jeffrey. *A Structural Study of Autobiography: Proust, Leiris, Sartre, Lévi-Strauss*. Ithaca: Cornell University Press, 1974.

Ménard, Jean. "*Le Paysan parvenu* de Marivaux." *Revue de l'Université Laval* 2 (Sept. 1956), 40-52.

Mendilow, Adam A. *Time and the Novel*. London: Nevill, 1952.

Merlant, Joachim. *Le Roman personnel de Rousseau à Fromentin*. Paris: Hachette, 1905.

Miller, Nancy K. *The Heroine's Text*. New York: Columbia University Press, 1980.

Miller, Stuart. *The Picaresque Novel*. Cleveland: Case-Western Reserve University Press, 1967.

MLN 93, no. 4 (May 1978).

MLN 94, no. 5 (Dec. 1979).

Molho, Maurice, ed. *Romans picaresques espagnols*. Paris: Gallimard, 1968.

Montabrut, Maurice. "*Tristram Shandy* ou les paradoxes de l'excentricité." In *L'Excentricité en Grande-Bretagne au 18e siècle*, pp. 83-100. Lille: Eds. de l'Université de Lille, 1976.

Morris, John N. *Versions of the Self*. New York: Basic Books, 1966.

Mylne, Vivienne. *The Eighteenth-Century French Novel*. Manchester: Manchester University Press, 1965.

————. "Structure and Symbolism in *Gil Blas*." *French Studies* 15, no. 4 (1961), 134-45.

Naves, Raymond. *Le Goût de Voltaire*. Paris: Garnier, 1938.

Olney, James. "Autos*Bios*Graphein: The Study of Autobiographical Literature." *South Atlantic Quarterly* 77 (1978), 113-23.

————. *Metaphors of Self: The Meaning of Autobiography*. Princeton: Princeton University Press, 1972.

————, ed. *Autobiography: Essays Theoretical and Critical*. Princeton: Princeton University Press, 1980.

Ouellet, R. and R. Bourneuf. *L'Univers du roman*. Paris: P.U.F., 1972.

Palache, John. *Four Novelists of the Old Régime*. London: Cape, 1926.

Parrish, Jean. "Illusion et réalité dans les romans de Marivaux." *MLN* 80, no. 3 (May 1965), 301-306.

Pascal, Roy. "The Autobiographical Novel and the Autobiography." *EIC* 9, no. 2 (1958), 134-50.

————. *Design and Truth in Autobiography*. Cambridge: Harvard University Press, 1960.

Perkins, Jean A. *The Concept of the Self in the French Enlightenment*. Geneva: Droz, 1969.

Perry, Ruth. *Women, Letters, and the Novel*. New York: AMS Press, 1980.

Pingaud, Bernard. "Je, vous, il." *Esprit* 26, no. 7 (July-Aug. 1958), 91-99.

Plaisant, Michèle. "Passion, sexualité et violence dans *Pamela*." *Bulletin de la Société d'Etudes Anglo-Amer. des XVIIe et XVIIIe siècles* 6 (1980), 37-59.

Porter, Dennis. "Fictions of Art and Life: *Tristram Shandy* and *Henry Brulard*." *MLN* 9, no. 6 (Dec. 1976), 1257-66.

Pouillon, Jean. "Les règles du je." *Les Temps Modernes* 12 (1957), 1591-98.

Poulet, Georges. *Etudes sur le temps humain, II: La Distance intérieure*. Paris: Plon, 1952.

————. *Les Métamorphoses du cercle*. Paris: Plon, 1961.

Preston, John. *The Created Self: The Reader's Role in Eighteenth-Century Fiction*. London: Heineman, 1970.

Rader, Ralph. "Defoe, Richardson, Joyce, and the Concept of Form in the Novel." In *Autobiography, Biography, and the Novel*, edited by W. Matthews and R. Rader, pp. 39-44. Berkeley and Los Angeles: University of California Press, 1973.

Richetti, John. *Defoe's Narratives*. Oxford: Clarendon, 1975.

Robert, Marthe. *Roman des origines et origines du roman*. Paris: Grasset, 1972.

Rogers, William S. "Marivaux: The Mirror and the Mask." *L'Esprit Créateur* 1, no. 4 (1961), 167-77.

Romberg, Bertil. *Studies in the Narrative Technique of the First-Person Novel*. Stockholm: Almquist and Wiksell, 1962.

Rosbottom, Ronald C. *Marivaux's Novels: Theme and Function in Early Eighteenth-Century Narrative*. Rutherford, N.J.: Fairleigh Dickinson University Press, 1974.

Rosenblum, Michael. "Shandean Geometry and the Challenge of Contingency." *Novel* 10 (1976), 237-47.

Rothstein, Eric. *Systems of Order and Inquiry in Later Eighteenth-Century Fiction*. Berkeley and Los Angeles: University of California Press, 1975.

Rousseau, Jean-Jacques. *Oeuvres autobiographiques*. Paris: Gallimard, 1959.

Rousset, Jean. "Comment insérer le présent dans le récit: l'exemple de Marivaux." *Littérature* 5 (1972), 3-10.

————. *Forme et signification*. Paris: José Corti, 1964.

————. *La Littérature de l'âge baroque en France: Circé et le paon*. Paris: José Corti, 1953.

————. "Marivaux ou la structure du double registre." *Studi Francesi* 1 (1957), 58-63.

————. *Narcisse romancier*. Paris: José Corti, 1972.

Rustin, Jacques. *Le Vice à la mode: étude sur le roman français de la première partie du XVIIIe siècle*. Paris: Ophrys, 1979.

Ryan, Michael. "Narcissus Autobiographer: Marius the Epicurean." *ELH* 49 (1976), 184-86.

Said, Edward W. *Beginnings: Intention and Method*. New York: Basic Books, 1975.

————. *The World, the Text, and the Critic*. Cambridge: Harvard University Press, 1983.

Sartre, Jean-Paul. *Qu'est-ce que la littérature?* Paris: Gallimard, 1964.

Schmitt, Richard. "Husserl's Transcendental Phenomenological Reduction." *Philosophical and Phenomenological Research* 20 (1959-60), 238-45.

BIBLIOGRAPHY

Scholes, Robert, and R. Kellog. *The Nature of Narrative*. New York: Oxford University Press, 1966.

Sgard, Jean, ed. *Condillac et les problèmes du langage*. Geneva: Slatkine, 1982.

Shapiro, Stephen. "The Dark Continent of Literature: Autobiography." *Comparative Literature Studies* 5 (Dec. 1968), 421-54.

Showalter, English, Jr. *The Evolution of the French Novel, 1641-1782*. Princeton: Princeton University Press, 1972.

————. "Symbolic Space and Fictional Form and the Eighteenth-Century French Novel." *Novel* 8 (1975), 214-25.

Shroff, Homai J. *The Eighteenth-Century Novel*. New Delhi: Arnold-Heinemann, 1978.

Shumaker, Wayne. *English Autobiography*. Berkeley and Los Angeles: University of California Press, 1954.

Sklovskij, Viktor. "A Parodying Novel: Sterne's *Tristram Shandy*." *Hasifrut* 24 (1976), 11-22.

Snow, Malinda. "The Origins of Defoe's First-Person Narrative Technique: An Overlooked Aspect of the Rise of the Novel." *Journal of Narrative Technique* 6 (1976), 175-87.

Spacks, Patricia Meyer. *Imagining a Self: Autobiography and Novel in Eighteenth-Century England*. Cambridge: Harvard University Press, 1976.

Spengemann, William. *The Forms of Autobiography: Episodes in the History of a Literary Genre*. New Haven and London: Yale University Press, 1980.

Spitzer, Leo. "A propos de *La Vie de Marianne*." *Romanic Review*, 44 (1953), 102-26.

Starobinski, Jean. "Le Style de l'autobiographie." *Poétique* 3 (1970), 257-65.

Starr, G. A. *Defoe and Casuistry*. Princeton: Princeton University Press, 1971.

————. *Defoe and Spiritual Autobiography*. Princeton: Princeton University Press, 1965.

Stauffer, Donald. *The Art of Biography in Eighteenth-Century England*. Princeton: Princeton University Press, 1941.

Steward, Philip. *Le Masque et la parole: le langage de l'amour au XVIIIème siècle*. Paris: José Corti, 1973.

Stewart, Philip. *Imitation and Illusion in the French Memoir Novel, 1700-1750*. New Haven: Yale University Press, 1969.

Suleiman, Susan. "Of Readers and Narratees: The Experience of *Pamela*." *L'Esprit Créateur* 21, no. 2 (1980), 89-97.

Swearingen, James. *Reflexivity in Tristram Shandy*. New Haven: Yale University Press, 1977.

Tamir, Nomi. "Personal Narrative and Its Linguistic Foundations." *A Journal For Descriptive Poetics and Theory of Literature* 1 (1976), 403-29.

Tanner, Tony. *Adultery in the Novel*. Baltimore: The Johns Hopkins University Press, 1979.

Thomas, Alain. "Essai d'analyse socio-critique d'un passage de *Moll Flanders*." In *Picaresque Européen: Actes*, edited by Edmond Cros. pp. 181-203. Montpellier: Centre d'Etudes Sociocritiques, Université Paul Valéry, 1978.

Thomas, Ruth P. "The Critical Narrators of Marivaux's Unfinished Novels." *Forum for Modern Language Studies* 9 (1973), 363-69.

————. "The Role of the Narrator in the Comic Tone of *Le Paysan parvenu*." *Romance Notes* 12, no. 1 (1970), 134-41.

Thomson, David. *Wild Excursions: The Life and Fiction of Laurence Sterne*. New York: McGraw-Hill, 1972.

Todd, Janet. *Women's Friendship in Literature*. New York: Columbia University Press, 1980.

Todorov, Tzvetan. "Les Catégories du récit littéraire." *Communications* 8 (1972), 125-51.

————. *Qu'est-ce que le structuralisme?* Paris: Seuil, 1968.

Trapnell, W. H. "Marivaux's Unfinished Narratives." *French Studies* 24 (July 1970), 237-53.

Tyson, Gerald. "The Rococco Style of *Tristram Shandy*." *Bucknell Review* 24, no. 2 (1978), 38-55.

Van Ghent, Dorothy. *The English Novel: Form and Function*. New York: Harper & Row, 1953.

Van Rossum-Guyon, Françoise. "Point de vue ou perspective narrative." *Poétique* 4 (1970), 476-97.

Wagner, R. L. "Quelques cadres d'études pour *Gil Blas*." *Information littéraire* 1 (1956), 29-38.

Walker, Robert. "A Sign of the Satirist's Wit: The Nose in *Tristram Shandy*." *Ball State University Forum* 19, no. 2 (1977), 52-54.

Warner, William Beatty. *Reading Clarissa: The Struggle of Interpretation*. New Haven: Yale University Press, 1979.

Watt, Ian. "The Recent Critical Fortunes of *Moll Flanders*." *Eighteenth-Century Studies* 1 (1967), 109-26.

————. *The Rise of the Novel*. Berkeley and Los Angeles: University of California Press, 1957.

Weinstein, Arnold. *Fictions of the Self: 1550-1800*. Princeton: Princeton University Press, 1980.

Weisgerber, Jean. "Formes rococo: littérature et beaux-arts." *Revue de Littérature Comparée* 218, no. 2 (1980), 141-67.

Wilde, Alan. "Acts of Definition, or Who Is Thomas Berger?" *Arizona Quarterly* 39 (Winter 1983), 312-50.

Wilt, Judith. "He Could Go No Farther: A Modest Proposal about Lovelace and Clarissa." *PMLA* 92 (1977), 19-32.

Zimmerman, Everett. *Defoe and the Novel*. Berkeley and Los Angeles: University of California Press, 1975.

INDEX

Adams, Henry, 23
Aléman, 33, 52
D'Alembert, 16
Altman, Janet, 70, 87n
Apuleius, *Metamorphoses*, 3
Aristotle, 15
audience, 71, 75, 84-85, 95, 97, 102,
103, 105, 109, 111, 119, 122-23,
131, 146, 147, 150, 160. *See also*
communication
Augustine, 26
author, 13, 23-25, 49, 70, 72, 82, 85,
104; versus narratee, 27; versus
narrator, 25; versus protagonist,
28
autobiograpahy, 11, 23-24, 57; and
fiction, 12, 24; "real" versus "fictive," 12-13, 23-25; in *Gil Blas*,
49-50; in *Tristram Shandy*, 128-
29, 130, 134. *See also* writing

Bachelard, Gaston, 19
Bakhtin, Mikhail, 27-28, 37, 61-62,
64, 73, 75
Bardon, Maurice, 30, 35
Barthes, Roland, 5-6, 14
being, 13, 18, 20, 21, 22, 39, 66, 119,
120-27, 141, 146, 152, 155, 159-60.
See also self
Benveniste, Emile, 4, 8, 13, 26-27,
41, 52, 156, 161
Bjornson, Richard, 47-48
Bony, Alain, 138n
Booth, Wayne, 128n
Brooks, Peter, 105n
Buffon, Georges-Louis, 16
Burney, Fanny, 10, 12
Butor, Michel, 4

Cartesian, 8, 15, 17, 18
Cibber, Colley, 82

Columbus, Robert, 60n
communication, 7, 102, 123-24, 132,
141-52; as social interaction, 144;
double communication, 75, 93,
96, 99-100, 102, 112-13. *See also*
language
Condillac, Etienne de, 8, 14, 15
consciousness, 17, 18n, 19, 20-21,
27-28, 61-62, 64, 89, 99, 124, 153,
154, 155. *See also* self
Corneille, Pierre, 125
Coulet, Henri, 94
Cox, Stephen, 14-15
Crébillon, 10, 29n, 36n, 44
Culler, Jonathan, 150

deconstruction, 20, 62
Defoe, Daniel:
  Moll Flanders, 9-10, 24, 27-28,
  35, 50-68, 75, 122, 124, 159; compared to Gil Blas, 53, 67; dialogism in, 62-63, 65; isolation in,
  51-52, 66; role-playing in, 51-52;
  selfhood in, 67-68
  Robinson Crusoe, 77
  Roxana, 9
Deloffre, Frédéric, 93
Démoris, René, 35
Derrida, Jacques, 6, 19n, 20
Descartes, René, 15, 16, 17
dialogism, 27, 61-63, 65
Dickens, Charles, *Great Expectations*, 58
Diderot, Denis, 16n, 104
disguise, 19-20, 24, 26n, 28, 37, 41,
44, 50, 58, 63, 65-67
distance, 29n, 30-33, 37, 71, 78-79,
89, 91, 96, 100, 104, 106-107, 110-
11, 122, 125, 138, 160-61
Donovan, Robert, 60, 64n
Doody, Margaret, 77n

189

Dostoyevsky, Fyodor, 9; *The Underground Man*, 64

Eagleton, Terry, 72n
Eakin, John, 23n
empiricism, 8, 15, 17, 20
enunciation/utterance, 4-9, 11-12, 27, 34, 37-38, 40-41, 45, 56, 65, 74, 102, 123, 130, 144, 156, 161
Epimenides, 6
epistolary discourse, 10, 69, 70-72, 79, 87-88
être/paraître, 119, 120-22, 124-27; in *Gil Blas*, 120-22; in *Pamela*, 120-23; in *Le Paysan parvenu*, 122-27; in *La Vie de Marianne*, 122-26

Fielding, Henry, 150
first-person narrative, 3, 4, 5n, 7-8, 13-14, 26, 57, 88, 129, 156; definition of, 9; function of, 10; versus third-person, 4-5, 11, 30-31
Folkenflik, Robert, 79n
Forster, E. M., 154n
Franklin, Benjamin, 23
Freud, Sigmund, 8, 113
Frye, Northrop, 12

Gasche, Rodolphe, 23n
Genette, Gérard, 9, 57n
Góngora, 44
Gossman, Lionel, 120n
Greimas, Algirdas Julien, 21

Hardwick, Elizabeth, 72
Heidegger, Martin, 18, 20-21
Helvetius, 16n
D'Holbach, 16n
Holtz, William, 141n, 144n, 150
Huet, Marie-Hélène, 30, 36n, 118-19, 126n
Hume, David, 15, 16, 20
Husserl, Edmund, 17-18, 20

identity, 6, 7, 14, 20, 25, 27, 29, 35, 38, 41, 48-49, 51, 61, 67, 96, 101, 108-109, 115-16, 118, 123-25, 159-60. *See also* self
imitation, 28, 34-35, 38-42, 49-50, 60, 62, 121-22, 124, 140, 157-58
irony, 28, 29n, 31-34, 37, 45-47, 48, 53, 74-76, 77n, 92-93, 106-107, 116, 131, 146, 154, 159

Jay, Paul, 23n
joke, 6, 22, 113, 127, 154-55, 157-61
Jugan, Annick, 103n

Kearny, A. M., 72-73
Koonce, Howard, 52

Laclos, Choderlos de, 10, 24; *Les Liaisons dangereuses*, 69, 80n
language, 13-14, 26, 46, 73-74, 77-78, 87, 111-14, 117, 120-25, 134, 140-42, 145-49, 157; social role of, 145-46
La Rochefoucauld, 90
Lawall, Sarah, 19n
Lazarillo de Tormes, 3
Le Sage, René:
    Histoire de Gil Blas de Santillane, 9, 10, 22, 24, 27, 28, 29-50, 51, 52, 75, 119, 120, 121, 123, 124, 126, 127, 157, 158, 159; mimicry in, 35, 38, 40-42, 121, 157-58
Laufer, Roger, 7-8, 24
Lejeune, Philippe, 24-25, 57, 68
Lévi-Strauss, Claude, 19n
linguistics, 13, 26, 122
Locke, John, 15, 16, 17
Logos, 7; divine, 17; pre-socratic, 20

McIntosh, Carey, 76n
Mallarmé, Stéphane, 6
Marivaux, Pierre Carlet:
    Le Paysan parvenu, 9, 10, 22, 37, 77n, 83n, 100, 106-19, 123,

124, 126, 127, 131, 159, 160; distance in, 106, 107, 109, 110-11, 116; multiplicity of selves in, 110, 113, 115, 116
   La Vie de Marianne, 9, 10, 12, 22, 30, 70, 71, 83n, 87-106, 109, 115, 119, 122, 123, 124, 126, 131, 159, 160; blindness, 88, 89; function of récit, 102-105; self-creation, 95-96, 102-103
mask, 21, 23, 28, 39, 44, 66-68, 72, 86, 92, 96, 97, 98, 99-100, 102, 111, 117-18, 120-22, 124, 127, 157
May, Georges, 3
Mendilow, Adam A., 129
memoir, 3, 34, 49, 50, 51, 52-53, 56, 59, 61, 63-65, 67, 69, 71-72, 87-88, 90, 95, 103, 107-108, 117, 119, 129, 131, 135, 157. *See also* epistolary discourse
memory, 11, 12, 15-16, 26, 50, 119, 155, 160
Merleau-Ponty, Maurice, 18, 19n
Metamorphoses (Apuleius), 3
Miller, Stuart, 33
mirrors, 39, 40, 42, 43, 45, 49, 51, 71, 94, 95, 99, 101, 102, 105, 117, 122, 127, 149. *See also* reflection
mise en abyme, 40, 86, 155
Montaigne, Michel de, 26
Montesquieu, 16n

narrator, 4, 5, 9, 10, 11, 12, 22, 30, 31, 156, 157, 158
   attitude toward protagonist, 21; in *Gil Blas*, 31-34, 45-47; in *Moll Flanders*, 29, 51, 52-61; in *Le Paysan parvenu*, 106-109; in *Tristram Shandy*, 130; in *La Vie de Marianne*, 88-94
   blindness of, 59, 60
   versus narratee; in *Gil Blas*, 29-31, 37; in *Moll Flanders*, 64-65, 74, 75, 76, 77n, 83n; in *Pamela*,

71, 87; in *Tristram Shandy*, 137, 146-47, 149-50, 152; in *La Vie de Marianne*, 101-102

Olney, James, 23n

paradox, 6, 7, 8, 9, 26, 97, 132, 133, 145, 156, 160
parody, 129, 131, 149, 151, 160
Pierce, Charles S., 20
performance, 21, 71, 84, 95, 102, 125, 144, 161. *See also* role playing
Perry, Ruth, 79n
Petronius, *Satyricon*, 3
phenomenology, 17-18
picaresque, 3, 28, 29, 32, 36n, 48, 51, 52, 61
Perkins, Jean, 14n
point of view, 5, 57, 65n. *See also* narrator
Poulet, Georges, 16, 17, 19n, 105-106
Porter, Dennis, 138
Preston, John, 147, 151, 154
Proust, Marcel, 26

reflection, 35, 37, 38, 39, 40, 41, 47, 48, 49, 51, 101, 102, 127
Richard, Jean-Pierre, 19
Richardson, Samuel:
   Clarissa, 10, 69, 70n, 72, 77, 80n, 82n
   Pamela, 10, 12, 22, 69-87, 94, 95, 113, 123, 124, 125, 126, 131, 159, 160; clothing in, 75-78, 87; compared to *Gil Blas*, 76; compared to *Moll Flanders*, 76; function of letters in, 70-74; public opinion in, 82, 83-84; self-creation in, 80-81
   Sir Charles Grandison, 69
Ricoeur, Paul, 18
Riffaterre, Michael, 150

Rimbaud, Arthur, 9, 161
Robbe-Grillet, Alain, 4
rococo, 7, 8, 9
role-playing, 37, 41, 43, 50-51, 52
    65, 70, 79, 84-85. *See also* disguise
Romberg, Bertil, 131n
Rosbottom, Ronald C., 90n
Rousseau, Jean-Jacques, 10, 12, 23,
    26, 58, 108, 143n; *Les Confes-
    sions*, 23, 24; *La Nouvelle Héloïse*,
    69
Rousset, Jean, 43, 44, 71, 88-89

Sartre, Jean-Paul, 18
Satyricon (Petronius), 3
Saussure, Ferdinand de, 19n
self, 15, 16, 17, 84, 97; as conceal-
    ment, 121; definition of, 8, 14; as
    distance, 111; eighteenth-century
    conception of, 16; and imitation,
    48-49; and language, 13-14, 18,
    123-24; and multiplicity of, 110,
    113, 115-16; and other, 11, 13, 22,
    65, 67-68, 97-99, 100, 105, 112,
    125, 131, 160-61; as other, 123;
    and phenomenology, 18-21;
    search for, 146; and self-creation,
    13, 95-96, 102-103; and society,
    11, 67, 122
semiotics, 9, 20, 41, 120
Smollett, Tobias, 10; *Humphrey
    Clinker*, 10; *Roderick Random*, 10
society, social: approval, 15, 126; as-
    cension, 11; code, 70, 120; condi-
    tion, 11; forces, 9; hierarchy, 34,
    35, 67; intercourse, 97, 144, 145,
    146; meanings, 120; position, 79;
    principle, 65; recognition, 124;
    situation, 32, 82; status, 39, 76,
    77, 83; structure, 49n, 77; success,
    32; values, 78, 120
Spacks, Patricia M., 76-77n, 146
Spitzer, Leo, 105-106
Starr, G. A., 24n

Stendhal, 23
Sterne, Laurence:
    Tristram Shandy, 10, 11, 12, 22,
    30, 52, 128; control in, 133-34;
    digression in, 134, 137-40, 155;
    history in, 148-49, 154-55;
    knowledge in, 148-49, 157; mul-
    tiplicity of readers in, 150-51;
    time in, 130, 131, 152-53
Stewart, Philip, 4
subject, 5, 7, 8, 9, 11, 12, 14, 15, 17,
    20, 21, 22, 50, 52, 72, 96. *See also*
    being; self
Swift, Jonathan, 150

Tanner, Tony, 82n
theater, 42-44, 82, 85, 88, 97, 106,
    109, 116. *See also* disguise; role-
    playing
Thomas, Ruth, 106n
Todd, Janet, 79n, 99n
Todorov, Tzvetan, 57n, 156n

Valéry, Paul, 9
voice, 10, 11, 28, 29, 33, 37, 48, 52,
    56, 57, 58, 61, 62, 64, 73, 90, 98,
    106, 156. *See also* first-person
    narrative; narrator
Voltaire, 16n

Warner, William B., 72, 81n
Watt, Ian, 52, 64n, 65n
Weinstein, Arnold, 67n
Wilde, Alan, 18n
writing, 4, 5, 6, 9, 10, 12, 13, 21; au-
    tobiographical, 11, 23; as copy-
    ing, 44-45, 50; functions of, 13;
    self-reflexive, 11; versus life, 25-
    26; in *Gil Blas*, 34; in *Moll Flan-
    ders*, 52, 58, 68; in *Pamela*, 71, 73,
    79-82; in *Tristram Shandy*, 130,
    131, 132-33, 149, 155; in *La Vie
    de Marianne*, 100-101, 102

Zimmerman, Everett, 60n

LIBRARY OF CONGRESS CATALOGING-IN-PUBLICATION
DATA

Laden, Marie-Paule, 1946-
Self-imitation in the eighteenth-century novel.

Bibliography: p.
Includes index.
1. French fiction—18th century—History and criticism. 2. First person
narrative. 3. Self in literature. 4. Imitation (in literature). 5. English fiction—18th century—History and criticism. 6. Literature, Comparative—
French and English. 7. Literature, Comparative—English and French.
8. Fiction—Technique. I. Title.
PQ637.F57L3 1987   843'.5'0923   86-25541
ISBN 0-691-06705-8 (alk. paper)

75368